Matthew M. Vriends, Ph.D.

Doves

Everything About Purchase, Housing, Care,
Nutrition, Breeding, and Diseases

With a Special Chapter on Understanding Doves

With 46 Color Photographs

Illustrations by Tanya M. Vriends
and Michele Earle-Bridges

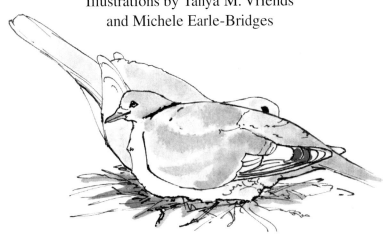

Contents

Preface

As both an ornithologist and a keen aviculturist, I find it hard to obtain sufficient information about wild doves, especially their behavior in the wild and their captive care and management. The available literature is sparse and often full of inconsistencies, especially on classification and geographical range.

My major reference on classification has been D. Goodwin's *Pigeons and Doves of the World;* for geographical range I have used H. E. Wolters' *Die Vogelarten der Erde,* Volume I. I have also added my own remarks and criticisms based on over 30 years of field research in various parts of the world.

In the species section I have used a fixed order of description; first, the English and scientific names, followed by the number of known subspecies. Then, Characteristics gives a brief description of the typical example, followed by mention of the subspecies.

Next, Natural Range and Behavior describes where the bird's native habitat is and what the biotope is like, plus notes on the natural food, voice, behavior, nest-building, egg numbers, and incubation times.

The third, and for the aviculturist most important, subsection is Care and Breeding, with information about first imports to Europe and the United States and, as far is known, the first captive breeding results. We note species that have never bred in captivity—a challenge perhaps for the serious breeder! Under this heading we also discuss specific requirements for care, feeding, and breeding.

By the seventeenth and eighteenth centuries, British and Dutch travelers to the East Indies had introduced to Western Europe the fantastic (now protected) crowned pigeons (Goura), the bizarre Nicobar pigeons (Caloenas) and many more amazing species. The zoological gardens of Amsterdam, Paris, and London must especially be mentioned for captive breeding of many species for the first time. Various individuals were also pioneers; for example: the legendary German ornithologist and aviculturist Dr. Karl Russ, who studied and bred various tropical doves in his laboratory. In France, the Marquis de Brisay, Vicomte Cornely, A. Decoux, Mme. E. Lecaillier, and Dr. Jean Delacour made their mark. In England similar advancements were made by T. H. Newman, Miss R. Alderson, the Marquis of Tavistock, and D. Seth-Smith. In Holland, A. E. Blaauw was perhaps the best known and most important breeder and fancier; he passed on much valuable information on care and breeding to the fancy. In the United States, the interest in doves began around the year 1918, just after World War I; names such as J. W. Steinbeck, H. Hecock, E. W. Gifford, C.O. Whitman, and C. A. Naether deserve mention.

I am grateful to Dr. Bob Dahlhausen, D.V.M., M.Sc., for the help he has given me, especially with the sections on disease and proper management; also to my friend, John Coborn, naturalist of Queensland, Australia, for his assistance.

Matthew M. Vriends

Understanding Doves

Doves in the Wild

Pigeons and doves belong to the avian order Columbiformes, and, with the exception of the polar regions, they inhabit almost every corner of the earth. The "headquarters" of the group, however, seem to be the Oriental and Australasian regions. There is no scientific basis for the separation of the words *pigeon* and *dove* though *pigeon* is often colloquially applied to the domestic, feral, and larger species characteristically having deep-chested bodies, small heads, and short legs (Family Columbidae); *dove* to smaller species. Of about 305 described living species, size varies from little larger than a sparrow to larger than an average domestic hen. There are small, dainty seed eaters and plump, robust fruit eaters. However, all doves have many anatomical features in common, and the group is quite homogenous.

Feral rock doves

Anatomical features: In general, the head is relatively small in relation to the body. The beak is also relatively small, short, narrow, and slightly bent down at the tip. The soft, sensitive, fleshy cere at the base of the bill is devoid of feathers. Only in the fruit-eating doves are the nostrils in the cere wide open and easily visible. The legs and feet usually have three forward, sturdy toes and one smaller hind toe, each with short, strong nails. The legs and feet are usually clearly scaled. In general, doves are either long and slender or short and plump, depending on the natural habitat. Various dove species possess so-called powder feathers. Using the

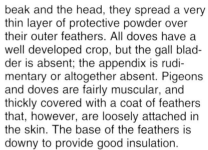

beak and the head, they spread a very thin layer of protective powder over their outer feathers. All doves have a well developed crop, but the gall bladder is absent; the appendix is rudimentary or altogether absent. Pigeons and doves are fairly muscular, and thickly covered with a coat of feathers that, however, are loosely attached in the skin. The base of the feathers is downy to provide good insulation.

Colors: The range of colors is quite remarkable: from milky white with black-tipped flight and tail feathers (nutmeg pigeon, *Ducula bicolor*) to blue-gray and white with a striking red breast patch (bleeding-heart dove, *Gallicolumba luzonica*). Various species are extremely attractive in their pastel or metallic shades of gray, fawn, blue, pink, green, and yellow.

Common behavioral characteristics: All species also have many behavioral characteristics in common. The whirring sound of the wings on takeoff is a trademark of all doves, as is their ability to suck up water through their short beaks in a long draft, rather than scooping and throwing their heads back as most other birds do. Unlike many birds, doves do not tuck the head under the wing when resting, but pull the head down between the shoulders. At rest, the healthy bird usually sits on one foot, the other drawn up into the plumage.

Reproductive Behavior

All members of the Columbiformes are monogamous, which is to say that they mate for life and remain true to their mates unless they are separated

The collared dove is an excellent example of how bird species extend their range within a short time.

permanently by some unforeseen event. Their flimsy nests consist of a platform fashioned from a few twigs placed loosely among the branches of a tree or shrub, or on a rocky ledge. In most cases the clutch consists of just two eggs, sometimes only one. The eggs are usually a glossy white, but a few species lay tinted (brownish) eggs. In most species both cock and hen share in nest building and incubation, but the hen usually performs most of the latter. The time of incubation varies from 13 to 19 days. The hatchlings are blind and naked and are fed by the parent birds on a special diet known as pigeon or crop milk, which consists of a mixture of partially digested food and a curdlike secretion from the crop lining (the dove's crop lining thickens during incubation). It takes 12 to 20 days for the young to develop sufficiently for fledging.

Pairing

With most dove species it is the hen who decides if a displaying cock will make a suitable mate. The cock begins his typical head-nodding displays at the beginning of the breeding season even when there are no hens around, but should he be spotted by a sexually ripe hen she will usually reciprocate the head nodding.

Many species of doves and pigeons allow their wings to "sag" when they are sexually aroused. This is done by separating the flight feathers so that the whole wing is partially open. This also exposes the markings on the back.

On perceiving the hen's interest, the cock will peck himself repeatedly behind the wings. If still interested, the hen will reach her head forward while the cock is still pecking himself. Moving closer together, the male utters his mating call and the female fans out her tail. Offering his open beak to the hen, the male will then rub beaks with the hen. Finally, the hen places her beak inside that of the cock in order to accept a gift of regurgitated food—or she goes through the motions of doing so. These actions, coupled with the mating calls, are the origin of the phrase "billing and cooing" and with the head nodding are very important parts of the courtship ceremony. Head nodding is used also during mating and as a form of greeting when the birds meet each other, especially during the change of incubation shift. Courtship often occurs near the prospective nest site and the head nodding is thought to play some role in the selection of a suitable spot. Observations have shown that a hen dove will mate more readily with a cock bird if he is in possession of a suitable nesting site.

The two young nestlings in a clutch (usually one of each sex), both in the wild and in captivity, are often attracted to each other and show it by conducting a pseudo-courtship ceremony. After fledging, this may even end in pseudo-copulation. The reproductive drive in doves is very strong. If pairs are separated then reintroduced, copulation may take place almost immediately. The courtship ceremony is almost dispensed with, though head nodding and billing may take place afterward!

The Nest and Clutch

Doves occasionally use the old nests of other doves or even other birds. Safety is the prime consideration. The nest is constructed in a hole, crevice, or ledge; among thick foliage; or anywhere predators cannot easily reach. Because many doves breed in colonies, they can warn each other when danger threatens.

The actual nest is constructed from small twigs, grass, straw, roots, and sometimes leaves. The building materials are delivered to the site by the male, and the female puts them together. At first sight the flimsy nest seems inadequate for its purpose. There is barely a cup—only an almost flat platform. The construction is often so thin that the eggs are visible through the gaps from below. However, the nest seems to stand up well and rarely fails. The hen lays her first egg usually in the evening after the nest is finished. The cock usually stays away from the nest so as not to attract predators. The female remains on the nest, but if she has to leave it she will hide the eggs by covering them with moss or twigs.

Though the cock usually assists with the brooding, he doesn't do much of it. He often takes over around midday, but by mid-afternoon the hen is usually back and continues to brood throughout the night.

Within an hour of hatching, the youngsters receive their first meal of crop milk. The chick's beak is taken into the beak of the parent who regurgitates the food. The finely ground food is given to the chicks for the first four or five days, but thereafter they begin to take more solid food. When feeding its crop milk the parent dove ensures that nothing is wasted; any that the youngster cannot swallow is reswallowed by the parent and offered again later.

Nest Defense
Although similar in many respects, the defensive behavior of many dove species varies somewhat. Generally, the dove stands motionless with its plumage flat against its body when danger threatens. Should an enemy approach from below the bird stands almost vertically, but if the enemy approaches from above the dove's body is held almost horizontally. When danger approaches a group of doves, there is a system of community warning; the first bird alarmed takes off with

A pigeon feeding its young. The chick's beak is taken into the beak of the parent bird, who regurgitates the food.

rapidly clapping wings, thus warning the rest of the group to do the same.

An incubating bird will stay extremely still on its nest as if hoping it will not be noticed by a prospective predator. Should the danger become too great, however, the bird will take off very noisily in the hope that the predator will be distracted away from the nest.

Feeding Behavior
Doves feed largely on seeds, berries, other fruits, green leaves and shoots, spiders, and various insects. They often travel great distances foraging for food for their young. The green pigeons (Treronidae) and the fruit-eating doves (Duculidae) (seldom kept in captivity), are wholly specialized in eating berries and other fruits, while the tropical ground doves (Gallicolumba), to which the bleeding-heart dove (*G. luzonica*) belongs, forage for insects, spiders, worms, slugs, and other invertebrates on the forest floor. The consumed food accumulates in the crop, a part of the alimentary canal that, in doves, forms a double sac. The main function of the crop is food storage, but it is probable that predigestion also takes place here. Doves possess two stomachs: a fore stomach or proventriculus, and a muscular stomach or gizzard (or ventriculus). The gizzard

The orange-fronted fruit dove (Ptilinopus aurantiifrons) comes from the western Papuan islands and inhabits lowlands up to 1,000 feet (300 meters), wooded savannahs, coastal woods, and mangrove swamps. They are known for their swift flight. They usually live in pairs or in groups of three (Goodwin).

Mating behavior of the bleeding-heart pigeon's male is very interesting: after several bows he runs after the hen, stops suddenly, depresses his tail, claps his wings, throws his breast upward and then bows his head forward.

grinds up the harder seeds with the help of grit. The fruit-eating species have a specially developed digestive tract in which the fore stomach is extremely large, the gizzard thinly walled, and the intestines relatively short.

Doves can be divided into three groups, depending on their methods of feeding:

1. Doves that obtain practically all their food from trees and shrubs.

2. Doves that obtain their food from trees and shrubs and on the ground.

3. Doves that obtain practically all their food on the ground.

Group 1 consists of doves that live mainly in the tropics and subtropics and include all of the fruit-eating doves: mountain dwellers of the genus *Gymnophaps,* long-tailed pigeons of the genus *Reinwardtoena,* and many *Columba* species. The food of these species consists of a rich variety of fruits, buds, flowers, shoots, etc. A few of the species are known to eat invertebrates, including slugs and snails (as, for example, the white-crowned pigeon, *Columba leucocephala,* from Florida and the West Indies). These species almost never descend to the ground in search of food, but will do so to obtain grit and minerals.

Group 2 contains a large number of species. They have a long, pointed beak to enable them to pick out delicacies from the foliage of trees and shrubs, or to poke around on the ground. It is believed that the Marquesas ground pigeon, *Gallicolumba rubescens,* from the Marquesas Islands of Fathuku and Hatutu, also uses its feet to scratch for food, as do gallinaceous birds (poultry, pheasants, quail, etc.); incidentally, this fact was first observed in an aviary. It is also interesting to note that in the wild, this species has been observed jumping up at seeding grasses, pulling down the seed heads and holding

Mourning dove eggs

them down with the feet so that the seeds can easily be picked out.

Group 3 contains various tropical and subtropical species that obtain practically all of their food on the ground.

Drinking and Bathing

Most dove species must drink once or twice a day. Fruit-eating doves were once thought to require no water, but I have observed many species in the wild drinking in the evenings before going to roost. The African ring-dove, *Streptopelia roseogrisea,* has a reputation of going for months without water, but this is extremely doubtful. I was able to observe this species in the wild during 1982, and at waterholes they gave me the impression of being "heavy drinkers." Most captive pigeons and doves will drink after feeding; there is no reason to doubt that wild specimens are any different.

The only species I am aware of that drinks heavily *before* feeding is the Australian crested pigeon, *Geophaps*

Pigeons bathing.

lophotes. Many members of the genera *Streptopelia* and *Columba,* and the diamond dove, *Geopelia cuneata,* drink before feeding their young, especially in older stages where the young are taking both normal food and crop milk. It has been observed that domestic pigeons deprived of water will become restless and will not feed their young. When water is offered they will then drink deeply before feeding the young. It is thus assumed that most species in the wild require adequate water when rearing youngsters.

Bathing: Some species like to bathe in the shallows or in a rain puddle where they spread their wings out over the water surface and splash water over their backs. Many species like to shower in the rain. Lying partially on one side supported by a wing, the bird holds the other wing high, in order to get its flanks wet before changing sides. Once the plumage is wet, the bird fluffs out its feathers so that the water can get right into them. After bathing, the birds dry themselves in a sunny spot.

Sunbathing and Preening

Many doves are extremely fond of sunbathing and will find a suitably sunny spot before spreading out the wings and fanning out the tail for maximum effect. Some species spread a single wing alternately, while others (only in the genus *Streptopelia*) spread out both wings as well as the tail. After sunbathing, the wings are pulled in, the feathers fluffed out and preening often occurs.

Feather preening is carried out with the beak like most other birds, but doves do not use preening oil, rather a feather powder that makes the plumage waterproof.

Dust bathing: Some species like to wallow in a sand or dust bath, especially on hot days; they spread out the wings and tail and scoop dust deeply into the plumage. This must have a cooling and soothing effect and probably gives some relief from parasite bites. After a dust bath the dust is shaken out of the plumage which looks all the better for its "maintenance." Many doves like to lie down on their belly after bathing or taking a dust or sunbath.

Doves clean dirt from the eyes by opening and closing the third eyelid, then rubbing the eye against the shoulder. The head and beak are cleaned and preened with a foot which, unlike with most birds, reaches directly to the appropriate spot rather than over the wing.

Preening and cleaning is often accompanied by peculiar stretching motions. One of these is known as the vertical stretch, a common phenomenon, probably designed to exercise the muscles and keep them in good order, just as we stretch ourselves from time to time. When fluttering the wings during and after bathing, doves often also stretch the body to its full extent.

The Voice

Some of the commoner aspects of social behavior in pigeons and doves have been discussed in the previous sections. With many birds, the song is an important accessory to behavior. Indeed, over the centuries the splendid voices of some birds have led poets to wax lyrical about them. Pigeons and doves, however, have been largely ignored in this area, since most of them have a very limited range of calls. Most of them "coo" with the neck stretched out. In spite of its obvious limitations, the dove's voice is used for many purposes, including contact, drawing attention to certain things, attracting, appeasing a partner, etc. In general there is little variance of call, even the mating call being similar but perhaps somewhat softer and "more passionate."

Cooing starts at a very early age and it is believed that it is an inherited rather than an acquired trait. In other words, "cooing" is not learned from the parents—it comes naturally. However, we must be cautious when saying this, as I have observed contact calls of many dove species (especially by hens as they arrive at the nest) answered by the young several days even before they have hatched from the eggs!

Adult doves have two major calls; first, there is the regular "cooing" tone that is usually uttered with the neck stretched up and the throat blown out. Second, there is the sharp, quiet tone that is uttered without inflating the throat. The unique whistling of the green pigeons (Treronidae) is a substitute for the cooings of other species.

Most species of doves have not more than four or five different calls. The standard call means much the same as the standard call of any bird that wants to mark out its territory and may be scarcely or clearly audible to the human ear. The contact call usually sounds practically the same as the standard call, as does the nest call, which is used by the hen when she arrives at the nest to feed the young.

Only when a bird is in pain or has been captured, does the call change to a sort of "growling" or "gasping" tone that can be described as "oerh" or "ierh." The call is used repeatedly by terrified doves and its intensity often depends on the size of the bird.

Defensive Behavior

If threatened or attacked, especially near the nest, a dove may stand its ground, spreading the tail feathers and raising one or both of its wings as if trying to make itself look bigger and more formidable.

The rock dove and some of its relatives use the stabbing motion of thrusting the head and beak forward in the direction of an adversary. Two birds using this motion will often both back down quickly and go their separate ways.

Head Nodding

Virtually all dove species practice head nodding, particularly as part of the courtship ceremony (see page 4). Some species, however, use this behavior as a form of aggression or defense while looking directly into the face of an adversary. When the head is lowered, most dove species expose certain color patterns on the nape. During the nodding display, the dove repeatedly utters its characteristic "cooing" call.

In many species the beak may almost touch the ground or the breast. The crowned pigeon has no special nape coloring but makes up for this by having a spectacular, fan-shaped crest. During display the crowned pigeon lowers its wings towards the ground and fans out its tail. At the same time the pupils dilate in order to show off the colorful iris.

All pigeon and dove species spread out the tail and usually raise it upwards at some stage of the head-nodding display. Tail spreading may originally have arisen as an impulse to escape; as threatened birds indeed spread the tail before taking off. Some species also raise one of the feet as part of the courtship display.

Flying Behavior

Doves exhibit a number of types of flying behavior, some of which are still poorly understood. In domestic pigeons the male often performs a display flight in view of his mate. This includes stretching his wings right out to make him appear larger and bringing them high over his back so that they clap together. These actions are often accompanied by an undulating flight and a spreading of the tail that clearly presents the markings on the underside. Goodwin has surmised that this flight behavior occurs:

The blue-crowned pigeon will often use a large basket or box fixed 3–5 feet above ground level. The species is a typical ground feeder but roosts high for the night.

• when the cock sees another pigeon flying;
• when he sees his mate or another pigeon performing this flight behavior in the immediate area;
• when he is at the point of flying away or returning to his cote after foraging for food, or after being transported and he is forced to fly back to his cote "under his own steam" (as in homing pigeons);
• when he flies in the company of his mate;
• immediately after copulation (in only 40 percent of the studied cases).

The Feathers

Doves have a full coat of feathers that is light and strong, protects the birds from inclement weather and skin injury, and helps in the regulation of body temperature. This plumage is very efficient and wholly suited to its function, insulating against cold in winter and heat in the summer.

The feathers can be classified into three different types: flight feathers, contour feathers, and down feathers.

Flight feathers are the primaries and secondaries of the wings and the large tail feathers. These have a strong shaft or rachis that runs right to the feather tip. The vane is the wide and the narrow side of the feather, consisting of a series of perpendicular barbs running the length of the rachis. The barbs interlock by a system of hooked barbules that give the vane a solid appearance. At the base of the feather near the skin, there is usually a group of free barbs that help to insulate, complementing the down feathers.

The feather shaft originates in a skin follicle that can be compared with the human hair follicle. The developing feather is supplied with nourishment by the abundant blood capillaries surrounding the follicle. The base of the shaft is called the calamus, where there is a round orifice that allows nutrients to

enter the shaft. When the feather is fully grown, this orifice closes.

Contour feathers are similar in construction to flight feathers, but have a weaker shaft that is much softer towards the tip. These feathers cover all parts of the wings and body that are in contact with the outside air. They streamline the bird during flight and protect against the elements.

Down feathers are very short and insulate the bird's body close to the skin surface. The barbs of down feathers are not joined by hooks, allowing the hairlike structures to spread out and form loosely matted layers. The bird can "aerate" its skin and tidy up its down feathers by fluffing out and preening.

Feathers are not evenly distributed over the body surface but occur in so-called feather fields. A feather field runs from the base of the lower mandible into the breast; here it divides into two more feather fields, one each side of the breastbone. These join near the ears and extend to the tail. There are no feathers in the wing and leg joints. A feather field runs over the head to the tail and another pair run from the thighs to the base of the tail.

The Molt

All birds molt periodically and doves normally molt once a year. The time of molting will depend on the climate, but in the northern temperate climate this usually occurs from about mid-July to mid-December.

In domestic pigeons and most other species the molt begins with the primary flight feathers. The new feathers start to grow before the old feathers fall out. This occurs when the new ones are about three-quarters grown. Groups of feathers are shed from each wing simultaneously, but not all feathers are shed at once, or the bird would be unable to fly. After the ten primaries are molted, the secondaries

begin their molt. Secondaries are not always all molted each year, but numbers may vary from two or three to all of them. The tail and contour feathers are molted at about the same time, the tail feathers one by one starting in the middle. The outer tail feathers are the last to be molted, by which time the new middle feathers are almost full size. The body feathers may be molted simultaneously in large patches so that birds may sometimes have temporarily bald spots, or even a bald head!

Down feathers are different in that they may be molted at any or all times of the year. In very warm weather, down feathers will be lost more quickly but are soon replaced as the weather cools down. The quality of down feathers can sometimes give indications about a bird's health. If a dove is not well the down feathers, especially those near the ears, are stiff and hard and not easily shed. This can be the result of disease, prolonged stress, or exhaustion from an over-extended breeding season. It is thus advisable to stop birds' breeding after the end of June.

Diamond doves are lively yet peaceful and easy to care for. However, when either a hen or cock is kept individually, it can be a nuisance, so it is important to keep them in pairs.

13

Molting is a natural process that will run normally in healthy birds. Young doves have their first molt a few weeks after fledging and it should be completed in 30 to 35 days.

Sometimes during the rearing of youngsters, the cock can become somewhat negligent because he is ready to start a new brood. This usually happens around the 14th day and can lead to so-called "growing stripes" in the plumage of the young. This occurs as a result of a disturbance in the feather growth due to erratic feeding. If this happens it is best to lock both parents in the shelter with the young until the first egg of the next clutch is laid.

Feather Problems

Doves occasionally have feather growth problems that can arise from sickness, damage, or dietary deficiencies. So-called "tube feathers" may occur when the membrane around the growing feather does not break. The barbs thus become rolled up in the follicle and can result in severe inflammation and even abscesses. Birds kept in optimum conditions are unlikely to suffer from tube feathers.

"Blood feathers" can occur if a blood vessel in or near the feather follicle is damaged, allowing blood to flow into the shaft. This condition usually rights itself after a while; so do not be tempted to pull the feather out! This may lead to excessive loss of blood. Damaged "pin feathers" (often called "blood feathers" as well) must be removed immediately (pulled out). Apply pressure to the skin opening until the bleeding stops.

Longevity

Captive doves live for a relatively long time when compared with their wild counterparts. In England a turtledove, *Streptopelia turtur,* lived in captivity for 34 years, while the famous passenger pigeon "Martha" was 29 years old when she died in the Cincinatti Zoo on September 1, 1914. In the Berlin Zoo, a spotted pigeon, *Columba maculosa,* lived for 25 years and a picazuro pigeon, *Columba picazuro* for 15. A Barbary dove, *Streptopelia roseogrisea "risoria,"* lived in captivity in England for at least 23 years.

Average captive life spans are probably somewhere in the region of 10 to 12 years. Naether had a female Key West quail dove, *Geotrygon chrysia,* that incubated (infertile) eggs at 12 years of age. This species has not been available in the trade since about 1945.

Acquisition

Getting Started: Before commencing your search, study this and other books on keeping and caring for doves. Also, read several issues of the popular bird magazines (see page 106) to see where you can most easily acquire the birds and supplies you will need. Fortunately, there are a number of such magazines that are well worth reading, and they all carry a wealth of advertisements.

Feel free to visit a number of bird stores, talk to the proprietors, and be sure to take good notes. Find out what the doves you like are currently eating so you can offer the same food. (If necessary, you could gradually change to new and better food by following the guidelines on page 27.)

Where to buy doves: Most pet stores strive to make their birds as comfortable as possible. The cages are light and airy, disinfected, and large enough to keep birds for long or short periods. As a rule, dealers really work to keep their collection of birds free of external parasites. But this is no easy task as new stock is constantly being brought in.

Note the condition of the cages, the food and water dishes, and even the perches. They all should make a neat, clean impression. If they do not, shop elsewhere even if you find birds that you like.

In addition to shopping at pet stores, consider buying doves from other fanciers and breeders. Newspapers and pet magazines are full of "Birds for Sale" advertisements—especially after the breeding season.

When visiting a private seller, the same points used for evaluating a commercial establishment should be noted. Everything should be clean and make a neat impression.

Tip: Don't buy mail order birds. Remember that no species of bird responds well to a long journey—even under the best of conditions. Also, there is no substitute for looking over the birds that interest you before you make your purchase.

What to look for: There are four basic points to watch for when shopping for birds.
• The birds should not sit with their heads constantly buried in their feathers.
• The birds should not fuss listlessly with their food.
• The birds' eyes should be bright and clear.
• The birds should have a tight covering of feathers (in contrast to sick birds whose feathers are parted and dull).

Don't buy birds that pick their own feathers or scratch between their feathers with their claws. Also, don't buy doves that have wet, dirty feathers around the cloaca.

Take a careful look at the breast bone. It should not stick out sharply in the front.

If you plan to exhibit birds, be sure that your purchases do not have missing toes or a deformed beak. Beak and legs should be free of injury.

Avoid birds that constantly rub their eyes against the perches or other furnishings. They may have colds, which claim quite a few victims among recently imported birds that have not been acclimated.

Bringing New Birds Home

If possible, buy small dove species early in the morning and try to have them home by noon. That way they can spend the rest of the day eating, drinking, and getting used to their new surroundings. Larger doves can be brought home later in the day.

In any event, get newly purchased birds home as quickly as possible. Small tropical doves can't do without food and water very long. But don't put water in the water dish—it would quickly spill out. Instead, provide a piece of water-soaked bread, which the birds will use to slake their thirst. Give them a small dish of seeds and/or fruit. You can keep seed-eating doves happy with a stalk of spray millet. Also, hang some spray millet in the cage or aviary when you arrive home.

If you transport birds by automobile, bus, or train, cover the cage with cloth or heavy wrapping paper. Leave only a part of the front uncovered to admit some light and air.

Precautions during winter: If you have to bring birds home during the winter (which I *don't* recommend) avoid placing them in a warm room immediately. The air in their lungs, air sacs, and hollow bones expands upon being heated. This puts great stress on the body and could cause a very painful death. Instead, permit the birds to get used to the higher temperature very gradually. This is the best way to demonstrate your concern for your cold birds!

Tip: Caring for more than a pair of birds is a time-consuming hobby. A well-managed aviary also requires real dedication and a considerable expenditure of money. Don't over invest. Buy relatively inexpensive birds to

Various mutations—pied, pearl, orange and ivory—of the collared pigeon.

start with (diamond doves or turtle-doves, for example) and gain experience with them. That way, you won't take the lover's leap too soon. Then, if you really get caught up in the hobby, you can make additional investments in the more expensive and harder-to-raise birds.

Housing

Introduction

Doves and pigeons like to have plenty of space about them. The larger the housing you can provide, the greater the chance of harmonious coexistence, without bloody battles, and improved likelihood of successful breeding. It is therefore obvious that the birds generally should be housed in roomy aviaries. Of course, there are some exceptions; the diamond dove, for example, will do well in a large cage. But the medium-sized species, such as Barbary doves and turtledoves, cannot settle in such limited space and should be kept in an aviary. Indeed, we rarely see such doves in cages today.

Space requirements:

Let us begin with some ground rules:
• Small dove species require an aviary with minimum dimensions of 6 feet (2 m) long, 3 feet (1 m) wide, and 6 feet (2 m) high.
• Medium-sized sized species require an aviary with minimum dimensions of 9 feet (3 m) × 6 feet (2 m) × 6 feet (2m).
• Large doves and pigeons require an aviary with minimum dimensions of 15 feet (5 m) × 6 feet (2 m) × 6 feet (2 m). Large species would include wood pigeons, fruit pigeons (*Ducula* and *Lopholaimus*), crowned pigeons (*Goura*), and similar birds.

The flight: It is very highly recommended to orient the aviary flight in a southerly or southeasterly direction; direct sunlight into the aviary, especially in the mornings, is of enormous advantage to its inhabitants.

Any aviary for pigeons or doves must have an attached rainproof and windproof shelter that can be gently heated in the colder periods. Shelter dimensions of 6 feet (2 m) square and 8 feet (2.5 m) high are ideal (for all three aviary sizes mentioned). You will have noticed that the suggested height of the shelter is greater than that of the flight. As doves almost always seek out the highest spots to roost at night, this will ensure that they enter the shelter to roost—especially important on cold winter nights.

The interior of the shelter should receive adequate daylight, so it is essential that large windows (with wired glass) are installed. The birds will avoid darker areas and this could be dangerous in the winter when the natural light is already subdued. The inside of the windows can be covered with a mesh screen so that the windows can be opened for ventilation in the warmer months, when it could get too hot inside the shelter.

Intruders: To prevent entry of vermin such as mice and rats into the aviary, the bottom of the aviary can be protected with a fine mesh buried 16 inches (40 cm) deep in the ground. You can use old wire mesh here as it will be below ground and invisible.

Cats can be a menace to your birds. I can still hear the furious cries of a fancier whose birds had been made to panic by a cat at night, causing the birds to leave their nests and indeed to abandon them. Although I quite understand his rage, it was good that he restrained himself from drastic action! You can stop cats from climbing up the

Bar-shouldered doves are very hardy and quickly become tame.

the safety porch and can easily be sent back.

Building an aviary: To avoid costly and time-consuming alterations after the aviary is built, prepare concise building plans at the outset. Remember that it is easier to alter a plan than to alter a building! Think of the following points: whatever the size of the aviary, it will be meant to last for many years. It must thus be durably constructed. Personally, I like to construct my aviaries, shelters, and flights on a low wall. This can be about 20 inches (50 cm) high, of which 12 inches (30 cm) is below ground level. It can be built of clay bricks, or more economically, from concrete blocks. You can cement upright bolts into the top of the wall as you build it, so that you have a really strong attachment for the aviary framework.

Access for the birds between flight and shelter must next be considered. You can indeed have a door in the wall of the shelter so that you have easy access between the two compartments, and it is quite easy to make a pop-hole for the birds in this. The pop-hole need not be too large; say 16 × 12 inches (about 40 × 30 cm) and it should have a sliding door that you can operate from outside the aviary with a rope, chain, or rod.

In colder areas it is advisable to line the walls and the roof of the shelter with a good insulation material.

When the aviary is finished, it is time for the paintbrush. The inside of the shelter is best given a couple of coats of nontoxic whitewash or a good white, water-based paint. White is best in the shelter as it reflects most light and brightens the interior. It also encourages cleanliness and helps you detect lice, mites, and other pests that may lurk in the shelter. The outside of the shelter can be coated with an outdoor wood stain that contains a preservative. It is available in various colors to

aviary mesh by spanning horizontal steel wires, at various heights, along the aviary about 3.5 inches (9 cm) from the mesh. A protruding edge to the roof will perform a similar function.

You can ensure even better protection by installing a nondangerous shock wire (electric fence) of the type used by farmers to control their grazing animals. However harmless the shock may be, a marauding cat, weasel, or other predator that gets a blast from the wire won't set foot on that patch again!

The one disadvantage of a shock wire is that the apparatus can be expensive. However, you sometimes see special offers in the bird magazines.

The door: It is advisable to have an entrance door to both the night shelter and the flight. The tops of the doors should be as low as possible, so that you have to bend slightly to enter. As birds tend to fly upwards when disturbed, this will prevent escapes. Even better, a safety porch can be constructed. This has a double door; on entering, you close the outer door before you open the inner door; you close the inner door before opening the outer door when you are leaving the aviary. If any bird should get out of the aviary itself, it will be trapped in suit your taste. Creosote, of course, is still one of the best wood preservatives, but I am not keen on using it. In my experience, the acrid fumes from creosote persist for several days and can be unhealthful for the birds.

Galvanized aviary mesh, especially when new, can dazzle your eyes and spoil your view into the aviary. You can greatly improve the view through the mesh by coating it inside and out with dark brown or black stain or non-toxic matt paint. The aviary framework, whether timber or metal, should be treated with preservative stain or paint.

Keeping the Peace

Most species of doves will live peacefully with other bird species in the community aviary, but often the mixing of species of doves, can mean bloody wars. With beating wings and pecking beaks, the fighting is fierce. Frequently this is a territorial dispute. Sometimes there are fights over the food station, especially in the breeding season. Species that normally live happily together can suddenly become the worst of enemies in the breeding season, especially over the food supply. Several breeding stations will often provide a solution to this problem.

Independent youngsters will be attacked by parents if the youngsters dare come into parental territory; they will be driven off with wing beating, and vicious pecks to the head and neck can even kill them. The aggressiveness of doves is often influenced by the amount of space they have, the amount of shrubbery, the number of feeding stations, the number of nesting facilities, etc. Birds also have variable personalities; some birds are friendly and docile, while others are born belligerent. New birds, therefore, must be observed very closely. Some of the more aggressive territorial species include the bar-shouldered dove (*Geopelia humeralis*), the bleeding-

heart pigeon (*Gallicolumba luzonica*), the crested pigeon (*Ocyphaps lophotes*), the Galapagos dove (*Nesopelia galapagoensis*), the Marquesas ground dove (*Gallicolumba rubescens*), the Soccoro dove (*Zenaidura macroura graysoni*), the speckled pigeon (*Columba guinea*), the white-throated ground dove (*Gallicolumba xanthonura*) and the zebra dove (*Geopelia striata*), plus all species of greenwing doves (*Henicophaps*), the green pigeons (family Treronidae) and the fruit doves (*Duculidae*).

Speaking of aggression, it is remarkable that the cocks of the bleeding-heart pigeon and the closely related Marquesas ground dove (sometimes called the gray-headed amethyst) will sometimes inexplicably chase and kill their hens. It is also difficult to understand the fact that the mourning dove (*Zenaida macroura*) is a docile, tolerant, and peaceful bird, while its very closely related subspecies, the Soccoro dove (*Z. m. graysoni*) is quite the opposite. The same applies to the aggressive zebra dove (*Geopelia s. striata*), and the peaceful dove (*G. s. tranquilla*), a fact that is recognized in the latter's English and scientific names.

Black-chinned fruit doves (Ptilinopus lectancheri) live in the forest of the Philippine Islands. They nest in trees or shrubs, and the hen lays only one white egg.

HOW-TO:
Aviary Maintenance and Furnishings

The Shelter
Roosting and perching sites: Many doves like to roost on a flat surface. Consider installing a 6-inch (15 cm) wide plank along the two longest stretches of wall. These should be as high as possible but allow the birds to stretch full height when they are standing on the planks. These must, of course, be regularly cleaned, and a wide paint scraper is ideal for this job. Perches of various thicknesses are also important, but don't overdo it! To prevent the birds fouling water, food, or each other, never place perches above one another or above drinking or feeding stations.

Nesting sites: Nesting platforms for the nest builders and nest boxes for those that like to be more comfortable can be affixed to the inside walls of the shelter. If part of the flight is roofed over (which is strongly recommended), nesting facilities can be provided outside. Many species of birds are keen on the fresh air and prefer to breed outside. If the nesting facilities are concealed behind shrubby cover, good breeding results should quickly follow. Nest boxes and platforms should always be placed fairly high on the walls, preferably higher than the average person.

Feeding, drinking, and bathing: Many fanciers like to provide feeding, drinking, and bathing facilities both inside the shelter and in the flight. There is nothing wrong with this as long as the stations do not become fouled with droppings. Many "green pigeons" (Treronidae) and fruit doves (Duculidae) seldom seek their food on the

Platform feeder.

ground and must have their water and seed hoppers placed on a platform some 3 feet (1 m) high. The stand should have a raised edge—about 1 inch (2.5 cm)—to secure the dishes (preferably heavy stoneware or the like).

The best way to provide a bath is to create a shallow pool. If you build a concrete floor in the aviary, it is a good idea to have the pool where the drain is. A plug will stop the water from running out until you want to clean. You then remove the plug and hose all the dirt from the aviary floor into the drain. Then return the plug and fill the pool with water. I recommend this type of bath, since doves have drowned themselves in a deep dish of water, especially when they are nervous—as when they have been shocked by a cat. In panic, doves tend to "lose their heads," with unpredictable results. For example, I once had a Barbary dove that always dived straight into the water bath each time I filled it with fresh water. He got so wet that he could not fly and ended

Wide plank for perching.

up in a corner on the aviary floor until he dried out. One summer night something must have scared him; I found him drowned in the bath the following morning. Doves are partial to a shower, however. They like mild rain, and a slowly running lawn sprinkler can also be a treat. Many species like to rub themselves against foliage after a rain shower.

The Flight

The Floor: The ideal aviary floor is smooth concrete, with a good runoff and drain. Living plants can be kept in pots or tubs. Worms and other infections can then easily be minimized if the floor is hosed down daily with a strong jet of water, preferably in the morning. The birds will soon get used to the procedure.

If your dove species like to forage on the ground, you could leave part of the aviary floor as natural earth. Or you could make a large, flat, timber tray—say 3 × 3 feet; (1 × 1 m) with an edge about 4 inches (10 cm) high, and place this on the floor of the flight. Place a strong plastic sheet in the tray and fill it with earth (preferably topsoil), which must be changed at regular intervals.

Natural earth floors must have adequate drainage. With rich soils like clay and fatty loam, which hold water for a long time, it is best to mix cinders with the top layer and cover with a 4-inch (10 cm) layer of coarse sand or gravel.

Perches: Perches, both purchased and natural, and of different thicknesses, should be placed at various locations in the flight. Take care to leave adequate free-flight paths, and for obvious reasons, never affix perches above feeding or drinking stations or, indeed, the growing plants. Some fanciers

plant shrubs that are native to the same habitat as that of the doves themselves, thus making an effort to partially simulate the natural biotope. Plant nurseries will be pleased to help you choose your plants.

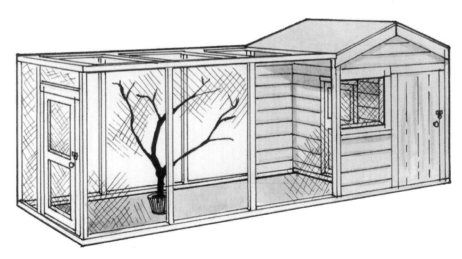

A small garden aviary suitable for doves.

In conclusion, we must ensure that aggressive dove species are kept only in single pairs; certainly not with more of their own species or with other dove species. Other bird species such as finches, parakeets, and gallinaceous birds can, however, be kept together with doves, usually with no problems. We must, of course, take certain facts into consideration: for example ground doves should not be kept together with pheasants, quails, or bantams, as such birds could quickly slaughter the dove with a few vicious pecks to the head. While on this subject it is worth mentioning that the young of some dove species may leave the nest too early and fall helplessly to the floor, where they can also become victims of other species. It is therefore perhaps best to keep gallinaceous ground birds together with doves only in very spacious aviaries, or to separate them from the doves during the breeding season.

You can see that some dove species do not deserve to be associated with the symbol for peace. Others, however, can indeed be peaceful and friendly.

Doves as Pets

The attitude of some dove species toward their keeper often also leaves much to be desired. Wild doves seldom become really affectionate to their keeper; they remain shy, nervous, and very cautious. Young birds that are born and reared in the aviary can develop a certain affection, but they are still always "on their guard." Newly purchased specimens, of course, must first get used to their new surroundings and keeper. Most of the ground doves (*Gallicolumba, Geotrygon, and Goura*) can become quite tame and trusting if they are given proper care and attention. Such birds will frequently learn to accept mealworms and other treats from the hand (especially if the treats wriggle), providing you are gentle, and the birds recognize you. It helps if you are always similarly dressed when you are dealing with your birds; many fanciers keep a special "warehouse coat" that they always wear when dealing with their birds. Never take strangers inside the aviary; and never allow dogs and cats a free run around the night shelter!

Choosing the Right Cage

When shopping for a cage, you will discover that a wide range of choices is available. However, not all models are suitable for doves. The cage must provide a proper home for your pets; style and elegance are of secondary importance.

Size: Only spacious cages in which the doves can move about freely should be purchased. Thus, the size

Multilevel cage for small doves

of your doves will determine the size of the cage. Apply the following rule of thumb: the birds must be able to flap their wings without running the risk of injuring their feathers. However, this is the *minimum* size that you should consider; larger is better!

Shape: In general, a rectangular cage is better than a square cage. Either, however, is preferable to a round cage, which can make your birds nervous. Avoid tower cages (the tall, narrow type). Doves are not helicopters; they are incapable of flying straight up and down.

Construction: Pay particular attention to the distance between the bars (or the size of the wire mesh). Many a bird has died a cruel death attempting to free itself from an opening that was just a trifle larger that it should have been.

You will also have to decide whether you want a cage with a single or a double bottom. The latter has a wire grating above a solid, pull-out panel—a most hygienic arrangement that is especially valuable in hospital cages. However, doves find the gratings difficult to walk on, so I do not favor this feature for everyday use. If you have a cage with a wire bottom, I recommend that you cover half of it with grassy sod. If the sod is sprinkled with water daily, it will remain green and the doves will bathe by rolling around on it.

Accessories: Water containers and seed dishes should be attached to the bars firmly and in such a manner that the birds cannot loosen them. Perches should be placed so that droppings will not contaminate food or water. All of the furnishings should be within easy reach of the birds—and of their housekeeper!

Box cages: A dove feels most at ease in a cage that is partially closed. The box cage, which has bars only on the front, offers birds a sense of security that conventional cages cannot provide. Ready-made models now available are often equipped with built-in lighting. Nevertheless, this type of cage should be placed in a bright location. Because of the limited ventilation, direct sunlight must be avoided. Box cages are eminently suitable for breeding (especially the smaller species such as diamond doves and turtledoves), precisely because they offer the nesting couple the most security.

Antique cages, which may sometimes be found in second-hand stores, can often look very rustic and may suit the decor of the living room or study. Generally, however, they are suitable only for the smaller dove species. If you wish to spruce up such a cage, use only lead-free paints that are deemed suitable for children's furniture. Pay special attention to the corners and other places where paint may collect (and vermin may hide). Birds can be placed in renovated cages only after all paint is thoroughly dry.

Location: As mentioned above, cages must have light and sun, but the doves must be able to escape from direct sunlight if they choose to do so. Rooms facing north are therefore totally unsuitable. The open side of a box cage should face south, if that is even remotely possible. When this is not practical, it should face southward. In this event, southeast is preferable to southwest. When the sun is too strong, shield the cage with newspaper or with a screen.

Height: Cages should be situated so that the doves can look down upon us. As you know, birds are accustomed to fly away from danger—a tendency they will display when they are approached by curious strangers. If the unfamiliar spectators are permitted to view the birds from above, your pets will feel they have no way to escape from potential danger.

HOW-TO:
Avoiding Danger

Possible hazards are listed below. Remedies appear in parentheses.

Bathroom: Doves can be poisoned by cleaners and chemicals or drown in an open toilet bowl. (Keep bathroom door closed.)

Cage and aviary mesh (with wrong-sized openings): the dove sticks its head through mesh or between bars, is caught, suffers injury, or strangles to death. (Check mesh size with pet dealer.)

Containers of water (sink, tubs, aquariums, vases): The dove falls in and drowns. Bird can mistake foam on the surface as a firm landing place. (Keep containers empty and/or covered. Bath water in cage and aviary should not be more than ¾ inch [2 cm] deep to prevent drowning [especially of fledglings].)

Direct sunlight, overheated rooms: Heatstroke: heavy panting, extended wings, weakness, collapse. (Get bird into shade immediately to prevent heart failure. Give dove some water and see an avian veterinarian immediately.)

Doors: The dove gets caught in them and is crushed or

Safe window with shade down.

escapes. (Close door before releasing bird.)

Drafts (open doors and windows, airing the room, etc.): Colds, nasal discharge, runny eyes, sneezing, pneumonia. (Avoid drafts; remove bird when room is being aired.)

Drawers, cupboards: Doves are curious and like to explore open drawers and cabinets. If a bird is accidentally shut inside, it can starve to death or suffocate. (Keep drawers and cupboards closed.)

Easy chairs, couches, etc.: Doves, especially fledglings, can be crushed when accidentally sat on. (Get in the habit of checking chairs before sitting down.)

Hard floors: Fledglings lack full powers of flight. Such birds can break a leg or bruise themselves in a hard landing. (Don't release young birds.)

Human feet: Free doves, especially fledglings, can get stepped on. (Look before you walk.)

Kitchen: Your birds are endangered by gas and cooking fumes. Fumes given off by overheated or burning teflon

Hazardous bathroom.

pans are toxic to birds. Also dangerous are steam and heat from cooking; open pots containing hot liquids; hot stoves; and household cleansers, all of which are potentially poisonous. (Keep birds out of kitchen.)

Knitted or crocheted items, yarn, string, chains: The bird's toes can get entangled; trapped bird can strangle itself. (Remove sweaters, yarn, etc.)

Large decorative vases: The dove can slip in and not be able to climb out again; suffocation, starvation, heart failure can result. (Fill these containers with sand or paper.)

Nicotine, sprays, etc.: Smoke-laden air is harmful; nicotine is lethal. Other dangerous air pollutants for birds are: paint fumes, carbon monoxide, insecticide sprays, deodorizer sprays, and insecticidal pest strips. (Do not smoke, use sprays, etc., near your birds.)

Perches too small in diameter; too many perches: Excessive growth of toenails; fractures. (Use hardwood perches of correct diameter.)

Pesticides: All pesticides are lethal for birds. Never spray plants in the room where your birds are kept or bring sprayed plants into that room.)

Poisons: Deadly: lead, rust, pans coated with plastics, mercury, all household cleaners. Harmful: pencil leads, inserts for ballpoints, markers, alcohol, coffee, hot spices.

Other poisons: acetone, amphetamines, aspirin, antifreeze, arsenic, bleach, carbon tetrachloride, chlordane, cosmetics, crayons, DDT, deodorants, drain cleaners, fabric softeners, firecrackers, fluoroacetates, garbage toxins, hair dye, linoleum, lye, matches (the so-called safety matches are nontoxic), medicines, mothballs, various wild mushrooms, lead-based paint, perfume, petroleum products, pine oil, rat and mouse poison, red squill, roach poison, shellac, sleeping pills, snail bait, strychnine, suntan lotions, thallium, warfarin, weed killers, wood preservatives. (Remove all harmful and lethal substances.)

Sharp objects, nails, splinters, ends of wire: Cuts, puncture wounds. (Remove all sharp objects.)

Temperature changes and humidity: Doves will do well at normal room temperatures with a relative humidity of 50 to 70 percent (60 to 70 percent during incubation). Outdoor birds suffer when the weather is cool and wet; a proper night shelter is essential. (Provide proper housing.)

Total darkness: Frenzied fluttering at night; broken bones or surface wounds. (Birds need 12 to 14 hours of natural daylight or artificial light [Vita Lite]. During the night use an 8-watt tube or a 15-watt bulb.)

Windows, picture windows, glass wall: Doves fly into them; concussion, fractured skull, broken neck, wings, or feet. (Lower shades; cover with draperies.)

Hazardous kitchen.

Covering the cage: Many fanciers believe that cages should be covered with a piece of cloth during the evening and at night. Not all doves, however, appreciate a fully draped cage. In my opinion, it is best to cover the side or part of the roof that will prevent artificial light from falling directly on the birds. They can then choose whether or not they wish to sit in the lighted area.

Cleaning the cage: The cage should always be kept spotlessly clean. This holds true also for the perches, the food, water, and bathing dishes, and all other furnishings and utensils. It is best to establish a regular routine for cage cleaning. Do it once a week at a convenient time. At least once a month disinfect everything with the greatest possible care. To do so you will have to remove the birds from their cages. (An extra cage, to be used as a temporary home at this time, will be very useful.) The primary cage is cleaned thoroughly with hot water, then washed again with warm water in which disinfectant has been dissolved. Use laundry bleach (e.g., Clorox) or buy a suitable preparation at the pet store. Be sure to read and follow the package directions. Finally rinse everything down with cool, clean water.

Golden-heart pigeon (Gallicolumba rufigula) on nest. This species has a quail dove shape and comes from New Guinea and surrounding islands. The clutch consists of one egg; incubation is approximately 29 days. The chick leaves the nest after 3 weeks and is fed by both parents for another 8 weeks.

Feeding

Introduction

The staple diet of most pigeons and doves consists of seeds, cereals, and legumes. In the wild, the birds seek their food mainly on the ground; to minimize the danger this can bring, they often forage together in groups. In such groups, when danger threatens, warnings can easily be passed on to all birds.

Feeding behavior: Pigeons and doves, like gallinaceous birds, do not dehusk their seeds before swallowing them. They usually go first for the larger seeds, as these contain the most food. They have to eat as much food as they can in the shortest possible time. The color of the food is not important, but the shape is. For example, doves are not fond of flat, or elongated seeds, nor will they accept seeds with a hairy husk. Next to seeds, cereals, and legumes, doves like some greens, such as lettuce, endive, chickweed, clover, watercress, shepherd's purse, and spinach. After feeding, doves like to drink. Little stones and pieces of grit that the doves have swallowed will help grind up the food in the gizzard.

Doves have to stay fit throughout the year; each season has its challenges. In the spring the cock and hen must come into breeding condition; both must be fertile, and healthy young must hatch from the eggs. In the fall, when breeding stops, the birds come into the molt. They must be fit and strong enough to fight disease at this time, when the weather can be very changeable. In the winter the doves are concerned with keeping themselves warm. Your doves must *always* have a balanced diet, depending on the seasons and what we expect from them.

A balanced diet: Compressed foods such as crumbs and pellets need not be used if you are able to give your birds a more natural diet. Seeds, cereals, and legumes alone are inadequate and must be supplemented with greens rich in minerals, grit, gravel, and, of course, water. It cannot be overemphasized that the water must always be fresh and clean (see page 30).

Obesity is one result of an unbalanced diet in doves. This can happen

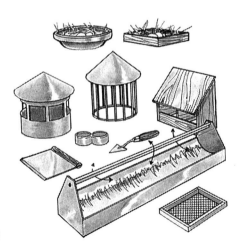

Equipment for doves and pigeons. From top to bottom: nest pans, seed or water container, grit or water pan, cover grit hopper, seed cups, scrapers, feeder, sieve.

if the food itself is unbalanced, or if the doves are finicky with their food, choosing too much of the wrong seeds.

Pellets: Before discussing the various seed mixtures, a word about pellets. Sometimes doves are fed with pellets or crumbs, which are manufactured as extruded diets. These extruded diets consist of milled cereals, seeds, and legumes, plus by-products of the granary and food-oil industries, and supplementary vitamins and minerals. Many feed factories became involved with this profitable business, and the market soon became saturated with substandard products. Most pellets were found satisfactory for homing pigeons and for breeding. One disadvantage of such foods in the past was that they led to loose droppings—probably due to the amount of molasses used in the manufacture. The compressing techniques were still primitive and a lot of molasses was needed to hold the pellets together. Molasses is rich in certain minerals and these probably caused the loose droppings. After a period of pellet feeding, it often became apparent all was not well with the birds. This could be blamed on a fault in the composition of the pellets. The layperson would, of course, be unaware of the constituents used in the manufacture of the pellets. Soon the pellets got a bad name generally, and gradually disappeared from the scene.

Seed mixtures: To give your doves a balanced diet, you must first know about the various foodstuffs, and how much of each is necessary. You yourselves can then make up diets for your birds.

Large amounts of cereals, legumes, and other seeds are used in the seed mixtures. The **grains** supply carbohydrates and are the main source of energy; they include buckwheat, groats, oats, corn, millet, wheat, and

rice or paddy (unmilled rice). They must be ripe, otherwise they could cause digestive problems. Rye has a bitter taste and is not generally accepted by doves.

In the **legume** group, peas, beans, lentils, vetch, shelled peanuts, and soybeans are the most important (see table 1, page 29). The most used **seeds** are hemp, canary seed, rape, sorghum, and sunflower seeds.

It is a well-known fact that cereals, legumes, and other seeds are not particularly rich in vitamins, which occur in changing quantities. You must therefore supplement to ensure that your doves get sufficient quantities of these vital nutrients.

It is advisable to use as few different seed mixtures as possible. The optimal mixture must contain all of the essential dietary constituents. The standard mixture should have a protein content of about 15 percent and an energy value of about 3,000 kilocalories per 2 pounds (1 kg) of food. The amino-acid constituent of the protein should be adequate for an adult (nonmolting) bird, as well as for a juvenile molting bird. In the winter, oil-rich seeds should be added to the diet; in summer, increase the carbohydrate-rich cereals. When youngsters are being reared and after the "pigeon milk period," include somewhat smaller seeds, grains, and legumes, so that the parents can feed these easily to their young.

Choosing the Right Mixture

Table 1 shows a summary of mixtures specially suitable for the larger pigeons (as in the genus *Columba*).

Ration 1 can be used as the summer diet for adult large species of doves. This mixture contains 70 percent cereals, which provides an excellent source of energy, and about 13 percent protein. If lentils and vetch seeds are difficult to obtain, or are costly, you may substitute safflower seed, and increase the percentages of soybeans and peas respectively by 3, 3, and 4 percent.

Ration 2 can be fed during winter, when you must offer a greater amount of oily seeds. The fat content of ration 2 is 9.6 percent, about two and a half times greater than that of ration 1. The doves need time to eat this ration as there are a lot of smaller seeds in it. It is therefore best to leave a light in the night shelter for an extra hour or two in the evenings.

Ration 3 is suitable for the young of larger species. The larger seeds (like safflower and corn) can be crushed. This food is thus first given to the parents after the "pigeon milk" period. A small amount of turkey- or pheasant-rearing diet can be given as a supplement. Fresh drinking water, greens, various-sized pebbles, and minerals must be available at all times. Vitamins can be dissolved in the drinking water and the bad taste can be disguised by adding a little honey. This diet should be given to the young throughout the rearing period.

Small Dove Species

Although good ready-mixed diets for small doves can be purchased, you can easily mix your own if there is no supplier in your area. By mixing together a good commercial budgie seed mix, a canary mix, and a wild bird mix, you will have an excellent mixture for your small doves. During the breeding period (and for some fanciers, the whole year) you can also give your doves some canary rearing food in a separate dish or hopper. Of course, you could also prepare your own basic seed mixture. Most doves of the size of a Barbary dove, turtledove, members of the genera *Melopelia, Nesopelia, Zenaida, and Zenaidura* (American mourning doves), the Australian bronzewings (*Phaps*), and similar

Table 1
Percentage Constituents of Seed Mixtures for Large Species

Ration	1	2	3
Beans	5	5	5
Buckwheat	5	2	4
Corn	20	20	15
Groats	5	10	10
Hemp	5	2	5
Lentils	5	—	—
Oats	5	20	10
Paddy rice	5	5	5
Peanuts	—	5	5
Peas	10	10	15
Rape	5	5	3
Sorghum	5	—	5
Soy beans	5	3	5
Sunflower seeds	10	3	3
Vetch	5	—	—
Wheat	5	10	10
Total	100	100	100

species will do well with a small seed mixture, plus grit, greens, and fruit (small berries, pieces of apple, pear, and similar fruit, depending on the season). Important seeds are: wheat, milo or sorghum, various millets, whole peas (Canadian, Australian), vetch, oats, groats, rapeseed, buckwheat, and hemp (especially during fall and winter). Very small doves, like diamond doves and masked doves, can be given a mixture of good budgie and canary mix. An extra shallow earthenware dish of hemp for tambourine doves is highly recommended; according to Dr. J. Nicolai, these doves eat lots of oily seeds even in their natural habitat in Africa. Over the years I have tried this, much to the doves' enjoyment.

The bronze-winged pigeon is generally an excellent breeder, if provided with an open nest-box fixed not too high in a thickly foliaged shurb.

Commercial pheasant and chick rearing crumbs can also be given as a supplement, plus finely chopped green food.

Ground doves of the genera *Gallicolumba, Geotrygon,* and *Leptotila* have a strong preference for dehusked sunflower seeds, finely chopped peanuts, milo or sorghum, various millets, small corn, a little softbill food (with insects; L/M's Finch, Canary, and Softbill Bird Food, for example), small pieces of cheese, chopped eggs, and commercial egg food (for canary/parakeet—the so-called rearing foods), good chick or pheasant: rearing crumbs, a rich variety of greens, and fruit (especially berries, chopped apple, and chopped pear). Live mealworms are a real treat, and each bird should be given three or four daily. As ground doves are extremely curious, they will soon learn to take a wriggling mealworm from your fingers and you will have tame birds in no time at all. Crowned pigeons need a similar menu, with the emphasis on fruits, greens, various cereals, soft (rearing) food, and insects (see page 100). Particular

requirements of certain birds appear in the species descriptions.

Vitamins, Minerals, and Trace Elements

Table 2 shows the most important vitamins. Today, most commercial crumbles, pellets, rearing, and soft foods contain the necessary vitamins. If the birds get adequate greens and fruit, a vitamin deficiency should hardly come into question. Nevertheless it is still advisable to give your birds a weekly dose of a commercial vitamin/mineral preparation in the drinking water or sprinkled over the fruit and/or greens. This can only be healthful during molt, breeding, etc.

Just before and during the breeding season, minerals are also very important. Therefore, sterilized, crushed eggshells—high in calcium—should be offered throughout the year. As you are no doubt aware, calcium has various essential functions: bone formation, muscle contraction, transmission of nerve impulses, blood coagulation, and eggshell formation, to name a few. If a bird refuses to take the eggshells, crush them to a powder that can be mixed with the seeds and/or sprinkled over the fruit and greens. It is necessary to give your birds daily access to crushed eggshells well before the start of the breeding season, so that the females are able to form the eggs. During the rearing of chicks, eggshells are important for the development of the skeleton and other parts of the body. Other good sources of calcium are oyster shell and grit, both of which can be obtained commercially.

Water

I make no excuse for repeating that doves require fresh drinking water *every day.* It may be given in shallow earthenware dishes. Doves, unfortunately, have a habit of sitting for "ages"

Table 2
Fat-Soluble Vitamins

Vitamin	Functions	Sources
A	Metabolism of body cells; maintenance of skin, bone, and mucous membranes; prevention of night blindness; synthesis of visual pigments.	Egg yolk; fresh leafy greens (chickweed, spinach, dandelion); yellow and orange vegetables and fruits; fish liver oils.
D_3	Promotes absorption of calcium and phosphorus; prevents egg binding; essential for blood clotting	Fish liver oils and egg yolk; produced in skin that is exposed to ultraviolet light (sunlight).
E	Prevents oxidation of vitamin A and degeneration of fatty acids; important for development of brain cells, muscles, blood, sexual organs, and the embryo; increases blood circulation.	Wheat germ and corn germ oils, fruits and vegetables, chickweed, watercress, spinach and kale, germinated seeds.
K	Promotes blood clotting and liver functions.	Green food, carrot tops, kale, alfalfa, tomatoes, egg yolk, soy oil, and fish meal; synthesized by bacteria in the intestine.

Water-Soluble Vitamins

Vitamin	Functions	Sources
B_1 (Thiamine)	Assists in overall growth; metabolic functions; growth of muscles and nervous system.	Germ cells of grain seeds, legumes, yeast, fruits, egg, liver.
B_2 (Riboflavin)	Egg production; metabolic functions; proper development of skin; feathers, beak, and nails.	Yeast, eggs, green leaves, germ of good quality seeds.
B_3 (Niacin)	Production of hormones; metabolic functions; proper function of nervous and digestive systems.	Peanuts, corn, whole grains, liver, lean meats.
B_6 (Pyridoxine)	Assists in the production of digestive juices, red blood cells, and antibodies.	Bananas, peanuts, beans, whole grain cereals, egg yolk.
B_{12} (Cyanoco-balamin)	Assists in the production of red blood cells; is essential for metabolism.	Fish meal, liver, eggs, insects, vitamin supplements (all plants are low in B_{12}).
Biotin	Assists in the metabolism of various acids and nucleic acid synthesis.	Egg yolk, nuts, greens.
C (Ascorbic Acid)	Assists in the metabolism of various acids, healing of wounds, tissue growth, and red blood cell formation; promotes absorption of iron.	Citrus fruits and juices, leafy greens, fresh fruits, cabbage.

Table 3
Amino-Acid Analysis of Crop Milk Protein

Essential amino acids	Percent amino acids in crop milk protein
arginine	6.83
cystine	1.24
phenylalanine	4.36
histidine	2.32
isoleucine	4.34
leucine	8.34
lysine	7.37
methionine	2.91
methionine + cystine	4.15
threonine	5.32
tyrosine	4.23
tyrosine + phenylalanine	8.58
valine	5.29

on the edge of the drinking dish, and thus fouling the water with their droppings. It can therefore be necessary to replenish the water several times a day. There are, however, "automatic" drinkers available that are generally quite good. The water stays clean and

These covered food containers can never be soiled, even when a bird perches on them.

free of potentially dangerous organisms for much longer, though it is still advisable to replenish the water at least daily. Ensure that such a drinker has a large, round opening into which the bird can thrust its head without danger of getting wedged. I have always had good results with the drinkers made for chicks and chickens, available in various types from good stock-feed stores.

Pigeon Milk
So-called pigeon milk or crop milk (see page 6) is unique to pigeons and doves and occurs in both cocks and hens. Wood pigeons feed their young with crop milk for about three weeks, and feral pigeons about a week less. Therefore, the chicks of feral doves can be reared by wood pigeons, but not the reverse. This is because feral pigeon parents start feeding solid food to their young much earlier than wood pigeons do. The results of various analyses of crop milk give a protein content of 10 to 18 percent (first results in 1930).

Engelsman (1962) found that dried crop milk had a protein content of 58.4 percent, a fat content of 35.1 percent, no significant amount of carbohydrates, and 6.5 percent inorganic material. What these percentages are in original crop milk can be estimated if the values for the dried material are known.

Harmuth (1971) analyzed the crop milk taken from chicks of wood pigeons (*Columba palumbus*), directly after they had been fed by adults. It had a dry material percentage of 27.55 percent, in which was contained 47.21 percent raw protein. This means that the original product contained 13 percent raw protein. The protein was further analyzed for amino acids. In Table 3 the results of this analysis are given.

Breeding Tropical Doves

Start With a Good Pair

In general, doves have adapted themselves well to civilization. Pigeons and doves form an important branch of aviculture; this is not surprising when one considers that dovekeeping goes back as far as recorded history!

It is generally accepted that a wooden board, a cigar box, a shallow basket, or the like is the ideal nest platform that will give instantaneous breeding success. Strangely, perhaps, this is not totally untrue, especially if such nesting sites are placed at a person's height among the twigs of a shrub, preferably in a sheltered, dark corner of the covered part of the aviary. It has been ascertained that nesting sites half filled with hay are more readily accepted by prospective breeding pairs. The structures that the birds themselves make are quite dilapidated affairs anyway, even in the wild.

But we must know more than these simple facts to be successful, because many species are not so easy to breed as one would have perhaps imagined. Over the years various methods have been developed and improved, and individual strategies are explained in the species section of this book.

Sexual Dimorphism

The most obvious requirement in breeding doves is that one must start with a good, compatible, and actual pair. This is not always as easy as it sounds, as in most species the sexes are very similar in outward appearance. It is often stated in the literature that the hen is smaller, slighter, and duller in color than the cock...but this can be taken with a pinch of salt.

Color dimorphism: When there is easily discernible color dimorphism in a species (the bronze-winged pigeon, *Phaps chalcoptera,* of Australia for example, in which the cock has a yellowish forehead and copper-colored patches on the wings; the hen a gray forehead and greenish wing patches) this is given in the species descriptions. But unfortunately, among dove species such differences are the exception rather than the rule!

Color dimorphism occurs in the following species: *Oena* (cape or masked dove), *Tympanistria* (tambourine dove),

A nest pan. Easily cleaned porcelain nest pans can be provided as well as paper nest bowls, which are disposable after use. The porcelain pans have the disadvantage of being too cold in the early part of the year; this, however, can be overcome with a thick layer of newspaper in the nest pan, then some tobacco stalks over the paper. This will act as a good insulator; as a bonus, the newspaper ink and the tobacco stalks help deter lice!

HOW-TO:
Breeding

Courting: Among the dove species, there is a variety of interesting courtship behavior before pairing takes place (see also page 4). Like dignified, strutting gentlemen, the cocks follow the hens about; cooing and nodding and pecking behind the wings, the birds perform the opening phases of their pairing behavior. The depth to which the cock nods or bows depends upon the species. When stretching out the neck to nod or bow the bird may let out a cooing call, but this does not apply to all species. Doves with glossy areas on the neck or wings, for example, will continually present these areas in the direction of the hen. A bleeding-heart

pigeon, for example (which has no glossy neck feathers), will set out its glossy wing feathers to impress the hen; its red breast feathers are also fluffed out to make the area appear larger and more impressive. Fluffing out of feathers to give an appearance of "bigger and better" is a common form of courtship behavior. Some doves also display the tail as a broad fan. Examples of doves that do this frequently are: wonga pigeons, *Leucosarcia melanoleuca,* and members of the genus *Geopelia.* The conspicuous naked eye ring (orbital ring) of many dove species, and the iris color also play a part in the stimulating optical display directed at the hen. In the wild (but not in the aviary) many species perform a courtship flight; especially in the genera *Columba, Streptopelia, Alectroenas,* and *Ducula.* The

cock flies in curves and circles around the hen, with spread tail and outstretched clapping wings, sometimes behaving like an expert stunt pilot! He always stays as much as possible within sight of the hen.

Another phase before pairing is the continual feather pecking that is frequently carried out with great gusto. Mutual beak touching and tapping is also a part of the courtship procedure. The cock often presents his open beak to the hen as if symbolizing the passing over of food. The hen reacts like a dove youngster and sticks her beak into his. The cock then makes regurgitating movements, but without producing any food.

Mating: After this stage of the courtship, the hen is ready to mate. She shrugs her shoulders and sinks to the ground and the cock mounts her. In some species the hen turns her head towards the cock; this also happens when we have two birds of the same sex! The courtship behavior itself is thus not proof that we have a true pair.

Nesting: After mating, the birds go looking for a place to nest. In the aviary, you must supply your birds with good nesting sites, bearing in mind that doves are not renowned for their architectural prowess! Even in the wild, eggs and young are sometimes lost through shoddy nest building. It is therefore important to offer good nest "foundations": for the smaller species like members of the genus *Geopelia* (diamond dove, for example) offer shallow wicker, plastic, or gauze, canary nest pans; for larger species a platform fashioned from mesh,

Nest boxes.

Bleeding-heart dove flashing wings to potential mate.

bark, or willow twigs is ideal. Wooden trays with the sides 1.5 to 2.75 inches (4 to 7 cm)—my personal favorite—can also be used. The hole-nesting doves can be provided with nest boxes as used by ornamental doves (see *Pigeons—A Complete Owner's Manual,* Barron's, 1989).

Placement of nest boxes: All species of dove that use nest boxes prefer them to be in the night shelter of the aviary (see page 18); for other species—in the shelter, in the roofed part, or in the open part of the aviary are all acceptable for nesting. Each nest platform or box must be securely fixed to a bushy twig or to the wall of the night shelter. If nests are placed in the open aviary it is perhaps best to cover that part of the roof with solid plastic or the like to protect the brood against rain and possible losses. This should pose no difficulties, as only a single pair of doves is usually kept in a (community) aviary (even doves of different species can be "difficult" with each other).

It is interesting to note that captive doves often nest successfully in quite strange circumstances. For example, Dr. H. S. Raethel, one of the world's best known dove experts, reported that in the Berlin Zoo a pair of pink-necked fruit doves, *Ptilinopus porphyrea,* from Indonesia (Sumatra, Java, Bali) raised broods year after year in a sand-filled dish. The hen lays just one egg per "round." The amazing thing was that the aviary was shared with about 40 lively and noisy lovebirds (Agapornidae), not to mention the daily thousands of human visitors peering into the nest. A related species, the black-chinned fruit dove, *P. lectancheri,* from the Philippines, laid her egg on the bare ground, even though "suitable" nest platforms were made available.

Nesting Materials: The best nesting materials for the smaller dove species include grass hay, coconut fibers, and moss; the larger species can be supplied with thin twigs—4 to 6 inches (10 to 15 cm)—of willow and/or birch, moss, heather, and straw. I like to place a thin layer of the nest material on the nest platform to encourage the birds to nest and to contribute to a more substantial nest.

Diamond dove on canary nest form.

Claravis (blue ground dove and purple-barred ground dove), the dwarf turtledove (*Streptopelia tranquebarica*), the emerald dove (*Chalcophaps indica*), the already mentioned bronze-winged pigeon, and some fruit and green pigeons (Treronidae).

It is incorrect to say that the blood-red patch on the breast of the bleeding-heart pigeon, *Gallicolumba luzonica,* is larger on the male than the female; nor is the male generally larger. The same goes for the blue-headed quail dove, *Staroenas cyanocephala,* from Cuba, which is known for its unique and interesting head movements, but both sexes are similar in color and size.

It is a well-known fact that with many species two birds will often behave as a pair if placed together, even if they are the same sex. You will soon know if you have two hens if three or more eggs appear in the nest—the normal number with doves is one or two! Two cocks together may sometimes spar or fight, but this is not always the case.

Determining Gender

The only way to get a positive decision is by blood test or endoscopic examination.

The blood test is a noninvasive procedure in which a single drop of blood is examined, and no general anesthetic is necessary. Since only a few laboratories carry out this test, you can obtain further information from your local avian veterinarian. Information is also available directly from Zoogen Incorporated, 1105 Kennedy Place, Suite 4, Davis, California 95616 or from Avian Sexing Laboratory, 6551 Stage Oaks Drive, Suite 3A, Bartlett, Tennessee 38134.

The endoscopic examination can be carried out only by a qualified avian veterinarian. Since many avian veterinarians are members of avicultural societies, they will usually do the examination for a reasonable price. The bird to be examined is anesthetized; the amount of anesthetic used will depend on the weight of the bird (we have given weights of species in the descriptions). The bird must have no food for several hours before the examination, so that the danger of regurgitation and suffocation is eliminated. After examination the bird should recuperate for several hours in a small cage in a warm, quiet area.

The advantage of endoscopic examination is that it can determine much more than the sex of the bird. By looking inside the bird's body, the veterinarian can make observations about its health, breeding condition, maturity, etc. The majority of tropical and subtropical doves must be at least ten months old before an endoscopic examination is attempted. Before that time the partially developed sex organs will be difficult to find or recognize.

Young Doves and Fostering

In general, we have said that various tropical and subtropical dove species are not difficult to breed, even when instead of using our well-placed nest platforms, they coolly lay their egg(s) on the floor! Some species don't like much disturbance (so be careful when inspecting the nest), while others have such a strong reproductive urge that they abandon one brood (whether eggs or already hatched young) in order to start another! In such cases it is worth trying to find foster parents for the abandoned young or eggs, although not all species are suitable for this task. In theory, the best foster parents would be of the same species as the young, but you would be extremely lucky to find doves at the same breeding stage as the parents of the abandoned chicks. You can only place them with the foster parents and hope that the young will be cared for. The best chances of success are when the eggs or young of the foster parents are at about the same stage of development as the abandoned brood.

Choosing foster parents: The following species normally make good foster parents: diamond doves, Barbary doves (my favorite by far), Senegal doves, spotted doves (for example Chinese turtledoves), and various fancy pigeons. Barbary doves have indeed played an essential role in the buildup of a good stud of white-bellied plumed pigeons, *Petrophassa plumifera,* which require a very large, thickly planted aviary if any degree of success is to be expected. Thanks to the pioneering work of the French dove breeder Delaurier (late nineteenth century) we can now breed bleeding-heart pigeons and other "difficult" species quite successfully via foster parents.

Apart from size (too large foster parents can suffocate the young of smaller species, especially in the early stages), one of the most important aspects of using foster parents in dove breeding is the type of food taken. For example, species that are mainly seed eaters are not normally suitable as foster parents for the young of fruit- or insect-eating doves. Thus Barbary doves can be used only for rearing *Gallicolumba* species if they themselves have been gradually adapted to a diet high in animal protein. This can be quite easily achieved by mixing one or more of the following with the normal seed ration and gradually decreasing the seed and increasing the protein: universal food, rearing food, hard-cooked and finely grated egg, finely chopped, cooked or raw, lean lamb meat (used often in Germany and many European zoos), a good insect food for tropical pet

Collared dove chicks, five days old.

birds (for example L/M's "Vita Vittles Canary, Finch, Softbill Birds Plus"), small dead mealworms, and skimmed milk solids (cottage cheese).

Preparing for fostering: The young of some species, such as those of the genus *Gallicolumba,* leave the nest before they can fly properly, and thus must spend time on the floor of the aviary. If the foster parents are Barbary doves, which are tree breeders, they must be placed in a low, long cage, with the nest platform on the floor. There are breeders who, encouraged by the fantastic examples of the American fancier J. Haffke, use three to five commercial chicken pens placed on top of each other. Each is divided into two with a mesh screen so that each compartment is about 12 inches (30 cm) high, 30 inches (75 cm) long and 24 inches (60 cm) wide. In the fall, at the start of the molt, the proposed pairs of foster parents are placed in a roomy aviary together with the pairs of the species whose offspring they will foster. Here the two species will become accustomed to each other and, with good care and management, will get through the molt without mishap. To prevent squabbling, never place two pairs of the same species together, rather one, three, or more (depending, of course, on the size of the aviary and shelter). After about two months in warmer areas such as southern California or Florida, or after five to six months in the colder wintry states, a pair of foster parents and a pair of the other doves are placed together in one of the compartments described above. You will have already installed two or three nest platforms in the cages so that the birds can make a choice (the choice also increases the reproductive drive). Optimistically, both females will soon begin their egg laying, and it is up to us to try and ensure that the egg laying is synchronized as closely as

possible. Of course, this is easier to say than to do, but we can lengthen the breeding time of Barbary doves by removing the eggs after four to five days. Usually they will lay a new clutch within 14 days.

Before giving eggs to the foster parents we should first candle them. In most cases the embryo can be seen after only two days of incubation. This consists of a small round fleck surrounded by a dark, beating mass. The embryo grows quickly and can be seen clearly by candling after 4 to 5 days, which is the best time to give the eggs to the foster parents.

Caution: the eggs of the foster as well as those of the other doves should not be older than four to five days.

Larger dove species can also be raised by foster parents, but we must still train the foster parents to take different foodstuffs if necessary. Many fanciers give their birds additional items such as pheasant pellets, crushed dog biscuits, boiled, grated eggs, germinating millet or canary grass seed. If using domestic pigeons (normally grain eaters) to foster members of the genus *Gallicolumba,* for example, it is essential that these foster parents must first be trained to take a large amount of animal protein foods in their diets. With the grain diet alone, the crop milk will be inadequate for the protein-demanding chicks, which will starve within the first week, despite having full crops.

Disturbances During Incubation

We have already mentioned that many species are easily disturbed when incubating. A good example is the bleeding-heart pigeon, which will leave the nest at the slightest disturbance, and then take a long time to return to her eggs or young. Luckily, there are also species that do not seem to be a bit upset, even if you put your hand under them in the nest and lift them to check the eggs or young! Examples of these "calm" species include all of the bronze-wings (*Phaps*), the crested pigeon, (*Ocyphaps lophotes*) and the bar-shouldered dove (*Geopelia humeralis*).

Of course, this does not mean that we take liberties with such species; always try and keep disturbances, and thus stress, to a minimum. So don't look at the eggs or the young on impulse. You can see how things are going by observing the parents. You will see that the cock and hen relieve each other at the nest so "professionally" that you have little chance of spotting the eggs or young!

So, be content watching the parents behavior. If this is normal, you can rest assured that all is going well with the brood.

Hybrids

A hybrid results from a cross breeding of two different species; unfortunately this happens all too often. It occurs especially in community aviaries in which several bird species (not necessarily all doves) are kept. Doves not necessarily of the same species (or even of the same sex) may become sexually interested in each other.

The "pure" aviculturist does not condone hybridization of any bird species. In most cases the offspring of such crossings will be infertile—so it is the "end of the line" for them. Neither the breeder nor the bird species is any better off!

Cross breedings also often result in death of the embryo before it even gets to hatch. Should hatching occur, there is a good chance that the hatchling will die in a few days.

By working together with other breeders, it should not be too difficult to arrange pairs from unrelated specimens of the same species. Offspring can later be shared, or some other mutual agreement can be reached. For the security of both you and your partner, written contracts are best.

Collared dove squabs in nest.

Collared dove squabs with pin feathers.

Collared doves, two weeks old.

Diamond doves are gentle, peaceable pets as individuals or in an aviary, even with waxbills and small finches. Remove all nests and nesting material to encourage the parents to feed the chicks until they are self-feeding; otherwise the parents nest again too soon and may neglect their offspring.

Diseases and Treatment

In general, doves are seldom sick, providing they are living in optimum conditions, and if all is well, they should live to a ripe old age (see page 14). In outdoor aviaries, however, doves can be infected by droppings or feathers of wild birds entering through the wire mesh of the flight.

If you are a conscientious fancier, you will know your birds well! On your daily inspections you will notice when something is not quite right. If a bird sits longer than usual in a particular spot with puffed plumage, closed eyes, and nodding head, or with dirty vent feathers smeared with thin, slimy droppings, it is time for it to be removed and placed in a hospital cage or other warm spot. Whenever you pick up a sick bird, examine the breastbone. If the area feels limp, and if the bone sticks out like a knife blade, this can indicate a chronic sickness. The next step is to get in touch with an avian veterinarian. As not all veterinarians are expert in aviary bird diseases, it is recommended that you contact the Association of Avian Veterinarians (tel: (407) 393-8901; fax: (407) 393-8902), whose address is on page 106, and from whom you will obtain the name of an avian veterinarian in your area.

Some of the better known diseases and conditions that may occasionally affect cage and aviary doves are as follows:

Pigeon Pox

This disease is caused by a DNA-virus: *Avipox columbae*. The virus is transmitted by bloodsucking insects and arachnids, such as mites, biting flies and, especially, mosquitoes. The pox infection can be acute or subacute, is slow spreading and characterizes itself by wartlike eruptions that form scabs, especially on the unfeathered parts of the skin such as the corners of the beak, the edges of the eyes, the nostrils, the ears, and the legs. Internal symptoms include yellowish diphtheritic patches on the mucous membranes. The pox virus can also be inhaled, and infection of the throat and upper respiratory tract can follow. One reason that bath and drinking vessels should be cleaned daily is that the water can be quickly infected with pox scabs or curdy exudate from the mouth. Contact infection can occur if the birds fight and the injuries are invaded by the virus. The pox virus can mature only in a wound or in traumatized epithelial tissue. Dry

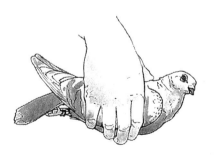

The correct way to hold a pigeon.

scabs, which can break into tiny particles, can retain live virus for up to 18 months! Latent infected doves (carrier) will shed the virus especially through the feces, but also via flaked skin cells and feather quills. It has also been ascertained that young doves hatching before the "mosquito season" are very susceptible to pox, probably because of their immature immune systems.

There are three forms of Pigeon Pox:

Cutaneaous: The skin or dry form. The lesions occur on the skin surface. A lesion starts as a small, blisterlike, whitish papule, but this can enlarge in a short time. Similar lesions are found on the skin of the eyelids, at the base of the beak, on the feet, legs, ears, etc. Eventually the lesions form scabs that fall off in pieces over a long period.

Diphtheroid: The so-called (and luckily not so common) wet form. Similar to the preceding form. The symptoms appear in the mucous membranes of the mouth, throat, tongue, crop, eyes, and trachea. Most of all, the symptoms are seen in the corners of the mouth. The blisters are raised, diphtheritic, yellowish-gray, and soft to the touch. In the case of an "eye pox," the eyeball is replaced by a cheesy, swollen mass.

Blood Tumors: Histologically this is similar to a pox virus infection with severe melanin accumulation.

An infected bird can have any combination of the three forms, but especially of the first two. Secondary signs include loss of appetite and the accompanying weight loss. Next, a cheesy, viscid, sticky material forms around the eyes and the plumage quickly takes on a stained, hackled appearance.

Sick birds must be immediately referred to an avian veterinarian; the still healthy birds, young and old, must also be examined, but separate the apparently healthy birds from the sick

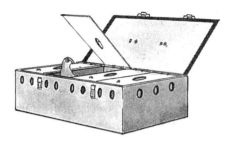

Transport boxes. The container must have openings to supply enough air for breathing.

ones. You can expect the sickness to last about 3 to 4 weeks. Water utensils can be disinfected with sodium hypochlorite (two tablespoons per pint). Add vitamin A to the drinking water and food. Good husbandry is the key here. Try to prevent mosquitoes "laying siege" to your aviaries. When the infection shows itself around the eyes, administer a few drops of mineral oil under the eyelids and give the infected eye a daily bath with 1.9 percent salt water. A systemic antibiotic treatment is recommended to prevent secondary bacterial infections.

It is also recommended that newly purchased birds be vaccinated. During the course of the vaccination reaction it is best not to give other treatments, such as worming preparations, etc. Vaccines should be kept refrigerated.

Ornithosis

Also known as psittacosis, this was once thought to be a disease exclusive to parrotlike birds. It occurs, however, in many bird species, including pigeons and doves, both in the wild and in captivity. The disease is spread in much the same way as a common cold, or influenza, by airborne droplet infection. The sick bird broadcasts the infected droplets by coughing, sneezing, or even wheezing, and the infected droplets are taken into the respiratory tract of the next victim. The disease is caused by an obligate intercellular organism, *Chlamydia,* and can be particularly virulent in unhygienic, stuffy, overcrowded conditions, as is exemplified by its high rate in imported birds, especially in those that have been smuggled.

The disease can have a variety of symptoms, and is usually difficult to diagnose in its early stages. First signs are often heavy coldlike symptoms, the bird wheezing and having obvious breathing difficulties. A runny nose, diarrhea, and moping are further signs. Later on, cramps and lameness will appear; if this stage is reached, fatalities are more or less inevitable.

Apparently cured birds, unfortunately, can remain carriers of ornithosis or psittacosis for the rest of their lives. Humans are susceptible to the disease, which is considered a serious hazard. Fortunately it is now quite curable with certain antibiotics (especially tetracyclines), providing it is caught in time.

Imported birds are now usually given prophylactic doses of antibiotics while in quarantine, and this has resulted in a marked decline in the incidence of the disease.

Salmonellosis

The *Salmonella* genus has thousands of different species of bacteria; most towns and cities, in fact, have their own strain! Some of the species can cause serious infections; *Salmonella typhi,* for example, causes typhoid fever, and many other species can cause food poisoning and various other enteric infections in humans and animals. In birds, including pigeons and doves, the rodlike *Salmonella* bacteria can cause various symptoms, and the disease is passed from one bird to the next via accidental or intentional ingestion of feces, or saliva (as in parents feeding young).

Salmonellosis occurs in four forms, which may occur in any combination:

Enteric Form: The bacteria colonize and attack the internal walls of the intestines. Digestion is severely impaired, and a green or brown, slimy fluid, containing undigested fluid particles is produced. This manifests itself in the foul-smelling diarrhea that is profusely evident in the infected bird.

Organ Form: If allowed to continue its course unchecked, the enteric infection will eventually make its way via the intestinal blood capillaries into the main bloodstream, where it can attack all of the organs in the body, including the heart, kidneys, liver, pancreas, and various glands, resulting in a breakdown of normal metabolism and ultimate death.

Joint Form: In the bloodstream, the disease will also attack the various bone joints, causing intense pain, swelling, and impaired movement.

Nervous Form: Once the *Salmonella* organisms attack the nervous system (including the brain, spinal column, and nerves), cramps and lack of coordination of movement will rapidly lead to death.

Remember, some strains of salmonellosis are infective to humans, so always wear an overall when dealing with infected birds, and wash your hands thoroughly after every handling session. You should do this any way after handling birds at any time; it will help protect your birds as well as yourself. All outbreaks of the disease should be referred to your veterinarian.

Trichomoniasis

This is a protozoan infection that causes caseous (cheeselike) plaques in the mouth, esophagus, and crop of doves and pigeons (especially adults), as well as other birds. Trichomoniasis is a common infection that must be combated by hygienic husbandry, including daily changing and cleaning of the food and water hoppers (use only recommended disinfectants, see page 47). Nestling doves can be infected by being fed crop milk by adults with the disease; the mortality rate in such cases is high. In general, it can be said that the main cause of spread of the infection is contamination of food and/or water by infected birds. Patients must be immediately referred to an avian veterinarian, who will diagnose the disease by examination of scrapings of accessible lesions and crop washings. There are various medicines used in the treatment of trichomoniasis, including Emtryl, Metronidazol, Flagyl (dimetidazole), and Ipropran (ipranadazole).

"Prevention is better than cure" is the appropriate proverb in this case!

Worm Infections

Various parasitic worms that can make life unpleasant for your doves and pigeons include roundworms and threadworms.

The roundworm, *Ascaridia columbae,* is white and about 2 inches (5 cm) long. It lives in the small intestine, reproduces quickly, and in a short time can cause serious compaction, in some cases enough to kill the victim. The thick-shelled worm eggs are passed out with the bird's droppings, and can easily infect other birds that ingest the eggs. The eggs can remain viable for several months on the ground. Once ingested by a bird, the eggs hatch, and the young worms attach themselves to the mucous lining of the intestine, where they can nourish themselves and grow to maturity. The cycle from the intake of eggs to when the adult female worm lays more eggs is about 30 days in young birds, 50 days in adults. Infected doves have soiled vent feathers, quickly lose weight, are generally weak, (especially in the later stages) and may show paralysis. Various vermicidal treat-

ments are available from your veterinarian, for example: thiabendazole, levamisole (in drinking water), or ivermectin (injection). Worming medications can be highly toxic and it is vital that instructions regarding dosages be carefully followed.

The threadworm, *Capillaria obsignata,* is a hair-thin worm about ¾ inch (18 mm) long; it burrows into the walls of the small intestine, causing swelling, inflammation, and eventual death. Like the roundworms, threadworms also are transmitted by feces and ingestion. The larvae develop into adults in about two weeks. A bird infected with a large number of threadworms will quickly lose weight, will make vomiting motions, and become anemic, emaciated, and listless. The bird refuses to eat and the head droops. Useful medicines include levamisole, Galinid and Tetramisol (the last two brand names are European products).

The tapeworm is a third kind of worm that mainly affects young doves. Found in the intestinal tract, these cestodes require secondary hosts (insects, earthworms, mollusks, etc.) to complete their life cycles. A couple of good medicines are Droncit (praziquantal), and Yomesan (niclosamide).

External Parasites

External bloodsucking parasites include mites, ticks, and lice; mites are usually by far the most serious. Doves and pigeons can easily be infested with red bird mites (*Dermanyssus avium*) if the feathers of wild birds drop into the aviary. Newly imported birds are also quite often already infested with various external parasites, usually evident in the "moth-eaten" appearance of the plumage caused by the birds' scratching and pecking at the irritations.

Mites: The red bird mite spends most of its time off the birds, hiding in cracks and crevices especially in the shelter, or near where the birds roost. The mites emerge at night to burrow in the birds' plumage and suck blood through the skin with their piercing mouth parts. Large numbers of mites can cause serious irritations, stress, anemia, and related consequences. The birds are kept awake all night because of the irritations, and thus sleep a lot during the day. They are then likely to skimp on their diets and lose weight. Untreated mite infestations can eventually lead to the death of birds!

After feeding on blood, the gray pinhead-size mites turn red; after getting their fill, they return to their hiding places in crevices, under cages, under nest pans, and so on. It is here that the mites breed, laying large numbers of eggs that can hatch in 48 to 72 hours when conditions are warm; this means that they can multiply in outdoor aviaries during the summer, but also in the indoor heated accommodations in the winter. Because of their mode of operation, mites often go unnoticed at first, at least until they have reached large numbers. They can be a particular nuisance during the breeding season, when irritation will cause incubating birds to leave the nest, and the young may leave the nest prematurely, often poorly feathered and weak. Sometimes mites can build up to such enormous numbers that if you stick a knife in almost any crack, you will pull it out with a blood-stained blade!

Fortunately mites are easy to eliminate. Many insecticides contain pyrethrin, an organic chemical produced from the pyrethrum flower, grown mainly in Kenya. The pyrethrin (relatively nontoxic to birds and mammals) is mixed with other ingredients that make it an effective insecticide or arachnicide (mites and ticks are not insects but arachnids—more closely related to spiders).

Red mite infestations can be confirmed by catching one of your birds at night and examining the plumage. It will be quite easy to see the mites running over the feathers, or even on your hand (they are no danger to humans). Another method is to place a folded white cloth near the perches in the shelter and examine it the following morning. If they are present, mites will have taken up residence in the cloth folds, and will be easy to see against the white background. Kill the mites by putting the cloth in boiling water.

To get rid of a mite infestation, you must remove the birds from the cages or aviaries, placing them in temporary accommodations. Spray every part of the aviary with a recommended solution of a good insecticide, paying particular attention to the crevices (in a well-built aviary, of course, these will be kept to a minimum). Wash water dishes and seed hoppers, nest pans, perches, etc. with boiling water. The birds themselves should be treated with a proprietary "body safe" pesticide that you can obtain from your veterinarian or pet shop.

Ticks: Ticks are similar to mites, but larger—up to ¼ inch (6 mm)—and tend to stay on the host longer. They drop off once they are full of blood. Ticks (occasionally found on newly imported birds) come in smaller numbers and you will rarely find more than half a dozen or so on a bird. A tick attached to a bird under the wing or in some other secluded part of the body can be removed by first dabbing it with a little surgical alcohol (in an emergency you can even use a drop of whiskey) to make it loosen its mouth parts. Then pull it gently out of the skin. Do not try to remove it without the alcohol treatment, as it will be likely to leave its head behind and cause a secondary infection.

Lice: There are several kinds of bird lice that may attack your doves. These are usually not as serious as mites, but can cause a lot of irritation and eventual anemia. Lice are insects that actually live on the body of the bird among the feathers and attach their eggs (nits) to the feather shafts or vanes. The lice may have biting or sucking mouth parts, depending on the species, but all kinds are just as irritating to the birds. Treatment with a proprietary pesticide as described for mites will usually effect a complete cure.

Wounds

Mechanical injuries, or wounds, caused by fighting and other accidents, are not strictly diseases, but do require medical attention. A bleeding bird should be caught immediately and placed in a quiet spot. Give it plenty of good food and some vitamin/mineral drops in its drinking water.

For bleeding skin wounds, apply firm pressure to the wound with sterile gauze until it stops bleeding. Then remove dirt, loose feathers, etc. with a pair of forceps, before dabbing the wound with a solution of hydrogen peroxide; do not scrub and probe the wound; this is likely to start the bleeding again.

For bleeding nails or beaks, use a moistened styptic pencil, silver nitrate, iron sub-sulphate, or a liquid coagulant, which must be applied to the bleeding spot. For larger beak wounds, consult a veterinarian.

During the molt, doves and pigeons may peck at the feathers. Since growing quills are filled with blood, profuse bleeding can result if the quills are damaged. As such blood does not clot readily, immediate action should be taken. Catch the bird and pull out the bleeding quill completely, using a pair of forceps, or even pliers in an emergency. Apply pressure as for skin wounds to the resulting cavity until the bleeding stops. In some cases you

may have to apply a blood coagulant, as for bleeding nails or beaks. Keep the recuperating patient in a warmed cage for a couple of days.

Commonly Used Disinfectants

Available through grocery stores, pet stores, veterinarians, and janitorial supply houses:

Lysol: manufactured by Lehn & Fials Products, Division of Sterling Drug Inc. Dilution: four ounces per gallon of water. All purpose disinfectant.

One Stroke Environ: manufactured by Vestal. Dilution: ½ ounce per gallon of water. All purpose disinfectant; official disinfectant of the United States Department of Agriculture.

Clorox: manufactured by the Clorox Co. Dilution: six ounces per gallon of water. May be irritating to the skin; may be corrosive to bare metal. Excellent for concrete flooring.

Betadine: manufactured by Purdue-Frederick, Inc. Dilution ¾ ounce per gallon of water. Excellent noncorrosive disinfectant, but more expensive. Obtainable through veterinarians.

Note: Always follow manufacturer's recommendations!

Basic Medications and Equipment

The conscientious fancier will have a stock of basic medications and other first aid items for use in emergency. This need not be elaborate, but many of the items listed can be lifesavers to your birds in times of need.

Important note: Keep in mind that most home treatments are palliative prior to the examination and subsequent suggestions of an experienced avian veterinarian.

Gevral protein, to stimulate appetite. Mix with Mull Soy (in ratio 1:3), which is also a good source of essential vitamins and minerals. The mixture can be administered with a 2–3 mm tube three times per day.

Glucose, as an emergency energy-giving food for sick birds that have not been eating. The glucose will quickly replace sugars lost from the body.

Kaopectate or Pepto-Bismol, for loose droppings and regurgitation. Soothes and coats the intestines and helps form solid feces. Two or three drops every four hours administered with a medicine dropper.

Maalox or Digel, for crop disorders. Soothes inflammation and disperses gas. Dosage: two or three drops every four hours.

Karo syrup, for dehydration and as a provider of energy. Add four drops to a 1 quart (1 L) of water. Administer eight to ten drops slowly in the mouth every 20 to 30 minutes with a medicine dropper.

Monsel solution or styptic powder, to stop bleeding—but don't use the latter close to the beak.

Milk of magnesia, for constipation. Do not use it, however, if the bird has heart or kidney problems. Three to five drops in the mouth with a dropper, twice daily for two days.

Mineral oil (liquid paraffin UK), for constipation, crop impaction, or egg binding. Two drops in the mouth with a dropper for two days. When administering mineral oil, take care that it doesn't enter the respiratory tract, as it can cause pneumonia, vitamin deficiencies, and possibly other problems.

For poisoning: Hydrogen peroxide, 3 percent activated charcoal, or milk of magnesia. Use to induce vomiting, to absorb the substance, and to speed its passage through the digestive tract. Ask your avian veterinarian for more details.

For scaly face or leg: Goodwinol, mineral oil, Scalex, Eurax, Vaseline.

For skin irritations: Betadine, Domeboro Solution, A&D ointment, Neosporin, Neopolycin, Mycitracin, Aquasol A. Domeboro is used on a wet dressing; dissolve one teaspoon or tablet in a pint of water. A&D is excellent for small areas. Neosporin, Neomycin, and Mycitracin contain antibiotics. Aquasol A is a cream and contains vitamin A. All these ointments and creams can be applied to the affected area twice daily.

Lugol's Iodine Solution, for thyroid enlargement (goiter). Half a teaspoon of Lugol with one ounce of water; place one drop of this mixture in one ounce of drinking water daily for two to three weeks.

Further health equipment would include:

Heat source, infrared lamp (60 to 100 watt bulb).

Hospital cage; several commercial models are available or you can make your own.

Environmental thermometer; buy one that is easy to read.

Cage covering; use a cage covering if you do not have a hospital cage. Towels or baby blankets are fine.

Adhesive or masking tape; use a half-inch roll.

Sterile gauze pads.

Cotton-tipped swabs.

Needle-nosed pliers and/or tweezers.

Scissors with rounded ends (baby nail scissors).

Feeding tubes; use 8F or 10F tube, which many veterinarians carry. Ask your veterinarian to demonstrate the technique of tube feeding.

Syringes or plastic medicine droppers, for administering oral medication.

The Dove (Pigeon) Species

Genera: *Columba, Turturoena, and Nesoenas*

These three genera, the members of which are all adept fliers, are usually placed together because they have many characteristics in common. Members of these genera are all of similar size to the rock dove, *Columba livia*, or the wood pigeon, *C. palumbus.* The main colors are gray (typically dove-gray) and brown. The neck usually shows a characteristic sheen and pattern that plays an important role in courtship.

Most of the species inhabit wooded areas and, with the exception of the rock dove, are thus not often seen in rocky or coastal cliff areas, although on the Orkney Islands they have to nest on the ground as there is nowhere else to do so. Foraging for food takes place mainly on the ground; though some species also forage among the foliage of trees and shrubs.

Members of the genus *Columba* are to be found in most suitable areas of the world, but in this respect it is important to note that biochemical studies have ascertained that the antigens (the substances in the blood that induce the formation of antibodies to fight invasions of disease-causing organisms) in the blood of doves from the New World are totally different from those of the doves from the Old World. In my view the relationship of these two groups is thus questionable, in spite of the general outward similarities of the species. Behavioral studies by the ornithologist D. Goodwin have shown that doves of the New World also have characteristics in common with the American ground doves (*Columbina, Claravis, Metriopelia, Scardafella,* and *Uropelia*)—an observation with which I agree.

Stock Dove or Stock Pigeon, *Columba oenas* (2 subspecies)

Characteristics: A small dove, smaller than a feral rock pigeon, but with a more robust appearance. The wide wings are somewhat shorter than those of some similar species, but

The stock dove (Columba oenas) nests in holes in trees, sometimes those abandoned by woodpeckers, but also in rabbit-holes or in sand or mud banks.

49

they are longer than their own tails. In flight, two black stripes can be clearly seen on the upper side of the wings (as when the birds are gliding to land), situated fairly close to the body. First impressions of coloring are that they are a somewhat darker and more intense gray-blue than the wood pigeon and, to be more precise, there is no white in the feathering; the whole body is dark gray-blue, with a reddish wash on the throat and breast. The primary wing feathers are dark brown, the tail is bluish-gray with a wide black edge at the tip. In contrast to the rock dove, the stock dove has a gray rump, and not a white one. Two short, black bands and the trace of a third black band can be seen near the top of the folded wings. The upper part of the breast is pinkish-purple with a beautiful full gloss, but not quite so large as in the wood pigeon. There is a glossy rainbow patch on either side of the neck; these patches sometimes meet at the back of the neck. The iris is strikingly dark and sometimes could be said to be black, depending on the angle from which one is looking at it. The eyes are a good indication of the bird's health; if they are light yellow-brown, you can be sure that the bird is sick.

The orbital ring, like the feathers adjacent to it, is bluish-gray. The beak is usually reddish with a yellow tip, but sometimes it may be dull white. The base of the bill is pink but the cere is flesh-colored.

The strong legs and feet are coral red. Although the sexes are difficult to determine, differences can be seen if you have adequate comparative material. I think the gray and blue of the hen is somewhat duller; the same goes for the feet and the beak. Length: 12½ inches (32 cm); weight: 8¾ to 10½ ounces (250 to 300 g).

Natural Range and Behavior: The stock dove, according to Goodwin, has an enormous range of habitat; a fact that also applies to other dove species. The stock dove occurs in western Europe, from Finland in the north to Portugal in the south; also in northwest Africa and eastward to Asia Minor, across central Asia to the wooded steppes of Siberia; southern Scandinavia, Persia, and parts of Turkey. Some northern birds like to migrate to warmer climates in the winter, sometimes traveling as far south as Sinai and the Nile Delta.

In view of the preferred habitat of this species, it is not difficult to assume that it was originally a forest margin dweller, from where it could take refuge in the woods if danger threatened. Today, where woodland is no longer so common, the stock dove likes to inhabit mainly open and cultivated land, often in parks, large gardens, and on the outskirts of country villages. In England they occur on cliffs and sometimes even in the larger towns. In England, the Netherlands, and Belgium they may be found among the dunes near to old buildings, and in farmland and mixed woodland.

The nesting site is very variable; I have found nests in tree hollows, in holes in walls, in chimneys, on the ground under shrubs, and once a free nest in thick foliage. In the literature all manner of nesting sites are recorded, including rabbit burrows, woodpecker holes, and artificial nest boxes. The altitude of the nest does not seem to matter as nests have been found in trees about 80 feet (25 m) up! Several pairs may often nest close to each other, in spite of initial squabbling as the nest sites are being selected. The nest itself is a simple platform built by both sexes from thin twigs and grasses. The hen lays two shiny white or light cream-colored eggs (40.1 × 28.7 mm) which have very thin, porous shells. Depending on weather conditions, two or three broods may be reared each season from April to July, though this is not a hard and fast rule—earlier and later broods are often recorded. New broods are usually started in a new nest site, as the youngsters can almost fill a nest hollow with their droppings! Both sexes share in incubation and the young hatch in 15½ to 16½ days. After a further four weeks, the juveniles are ready to leave the nest.

Once fully feathered, the juveniles are very similar in appearance to the adults, but are generally somewhat duller in color, while the breast is rusty-yellow-brown and the beak and the feet are dark gray-black. The green also is absent from the sides of the neck. The young cocks' feet color into pink after three weeks.

I would like to make a few more remarks about this species. Observed in the field, the stock dove can be distinguished from the wood pigeon by its darker, uniform gray-blue color. The stock dove flies faster, with more wing beats than the wood pigeon, but not quite as fast as the rock dove and its feral cousins. I also have the impression that the stock dove flies with its beak held lower than the other two species mentioned. But this can only be determined after one has had many opportunities of studying all three species in the field.

The voice is easy to distinguish from that of the other two species. The call sounds like "coo-ou, wou" (ou as in you) with the accent on the first note. The call may be repeated monotonously four to ten times. The same call is used as a nest call. During the courtship dance the call is repeated very softly and, if you are close by, you may also hear a distinct click. This could be vocal, but is more likely to be the mandibles of the beak clicking together. But bear in mind that doves normally call with the beak closed!

The courtship dance is very similar to that of the wood pigeon, with much head nodding and the tail spread out on the ground. The display flight is also similar to that of the wood pigeon, though perhaps not quite so pronounced. Both birds glide together horizontally with the occasional wing-beat. Copulation is also similar to that of the wood pigeon, but the cock continues to nod and bow while the hen remains still. The cock may continue to bow after pairing is completed.

Care and Breeding: These doves make ideal pets. They are very hardy, but in outdoor aviaries they should still have access to a draft-proof and damp-proof shelter. They are normally quite peaceful, are monogamous, and can be regarded as almost affectionate towards their keeper; moreover they often live for 15 years or longer.

The stock dove is being bred in increasing numbers in many parts of the world. Three to four broods per season are not unusual. An ideal nest box size is 14 × 14 × 18 inches (approx. 36 × 36 × 46 cm), with an entrance hole 4⅓ inches (11 cm) in diameter. The box should be affixed—preferably in the night shelter or roofed part of the aviary—so that the birds have adequate space to sit on top of it and survey the surroundings. Once the young have fledged, a new, clean nest box must be made available for the next brood.

The stock dove finds almost all of its food by foraging on the ground. It is an active bird, running hither and thither, tasting and eating. In addition to a great variety of wild seeds, the stock dove also takes cultivated seeds; a fact that makes this bird unpopular with farmers! The stock dove also takes slugs, small insects, as well as germinated seeds, pieces of living leaves, buds, shoots, and roots. The last four items are not eaten as frequently as the wood pigeon eats them (bear in mind that these are the wood pigeon's staple diet).

It is questionable if the stock dove eats berries, acorns and/or beechnuts. I have never observed that they do so; I agree with the dove expert Derek Goodwin in this respect.

Both sexes are known for their courageous and aggressive nest defending (at least for doves), and larger birds as well as other doves are driven off fiercely with much wing clapping and pecking.

Wood Pigeon (*Columba palumbus*) (5 subspecies)

(Other names: Ring Dove, Cusshat, Cushadoo, Quest, Ring Pigeon, and Stock Dove)

Characteristics: This species is somewhat larger than the feral rock pigeon. A common pigeon, it is not the pest that is frequently described and is,

The wood pigeon (Columba palumbus) is closely related to the stock dove, and has a white bar on the wing and white patches on either side of the metallic green neck.

indeed, a great aviary bird. The wood pigeon has a pleasant voice and attractive plumage on its almost round body. The wings are not as long as those of the rock pigeon; the same applies to the legs. The tail, however, is longer than that of the rock pigeon. The broad, white wing bands are conspicuous when the bird is resting as much as when it is flying. The sides of the neck show a purple and green sheen, and the white neck marking is one of the most characteristic features of this species. The rump and the upper tail feathers are dove-gray and there is a broad black band at the end of the tail.

The iris may be greenish-white to pale gold, but mostly pale lemon yellow. The legs and feet are dark reddish-purple. The naked orbital ring is gray. The beak is yellowish-gold with a pink-purple base. The cere is whitish.

Juveniles are similar to the adults, but do not have the white neck markings and are altogether duller in tint. Adult cocks and hens are almost identical in color, but the cocks tend to have more white on the neck and more pink on the breast.

The subspecies *C. p. iranica,* occurs in Persia. This bird has an almost white, or pale yellow beak; the north Indian race, *C. p. casiotis,* has creamy brownish-yellow neck markings. The North African form has paler neck markings, while those from Madeira and the Azores (*C. p. madarensis,* and *C. p. azorica*) have dull and small neck markings.

The wood pigeon is easy to identify in flight by the white wing bands. While resting, the neck markings and the long tail are good identifying features. Another characteristic of this species is its habit of lightly spreading and moving its tail up and down before taking wing. Length: 16⅛ inches (41 cm); weight: 17⅝ ounces (500 g).

Natural Range and Behavior: In Europe, the wood pigeon occurs in the north to about 66 degrees N., and through to Iran and northern India; also eastern and central Azores, the mountain forests of Madeira (where, according to Goodwin, the birds are now extinct) and finally, the mountain woodlands of northwest Africa. Although the bird was originally a woodland species (as its name suggests) it has, over the years, changed its habits in many parts of its range, often becoming an inhabitant of cultivated areas (farms, parks, larger gardens, etc.), sometimes even in the larger cities. In areas where suitable trees are scarce, on the Orkney Islands, for example, the birds will often nest on the ground.

Wood pigeons that occur in northern Europe often winter in central Europe, more often in the western parts. In the Netherlands and Belgium, for example, they travel through in great numbers during the months of October and November, and February to May. In the Netherlands, as well as in its southern neighboring country Belgium, the wood pigeon is a very abundant breeding bird—even in the towns and villages.

The wood pigeon does not use old nests of crows or other birds; it builds a shallow nest with twigs, often so flimsy that you can see the eggs through the twigs from below! Although the nests are usually built in trees or shrubs, the town-dwelling pigeons will often nest on the ledges of buildings. The nests are very occasionally found in tree or rock hollows or on the ground.

The wood pigeon can breed as early as March, and continue through to October, but the main season is usually from June to mid-September. The hen lays 2 to 3 thin-shelled, roughly textured, shiny, white eggs (40.1 × 28.7 mm). The incubation time is 15½ to 17½ days. Both sexes incubate. The young fledge after 20 to 25 days.

Incubation begins after the second egg is laid, thus usually after the whole clutch is laid. Nests found with more than the usual numbers of eggs are usually those shared by two or more hens.

Outside the breeding season wood pigeons are fairly sociable and will often forage together and even roost together in groups. But pairs remain faithful to each other and split off into territories for breeding. At such times they will fiercely defend their territories against intruders. Occasionally males will roost together when their hens are incubating overnight.

The courtship dance is very interesting. The cock usually begins the ceremony by bowing the head several times, while his neck feathers are fluffed out, showing off the markings and accentuating his golden beak and his pale-colored eyes. During the display, the pupils contract to mere dots. The tail is raised and fanned out, peacocklike, then is slowly brought down; the phase is finished with another head bow. The tail spreading is not performed if the prospective partner is not interested or hardly interested or runs away. In flight, the cock claps his wings together loudly before gliding in a shallow downward bow, with almost horizontally outstretched wings (markedly different from the stock and rock pigeons with their wings only partly stretched out). After two or three of these displays, the cock lands again on a branch or the like. Often a little "billing" takes place after such a display, the cock spreading his neck feathers again just before copulation begins.

The musical voice, sometimes loud, but usually a soft "coo, coo, coo; roocoo," is used in the display flight, also as the bird takes off with much wing clapping. The voice is much softer when the bird is resting on a branch.

The ashy wood pigeon or blue ground dove feeds largely on the ground and is found in Mexico, Peru, Bolivia, northern Argentina and southern Brazil.

Wood pigeons have a very varied diet that includes leaf buds, young leaves, grass and other plant seeds, various cereals and nuts, assorted berries, and, for a change, small invertebrates such as green caterpillars, slugs, and even the occasional earthworm. In agricultural areas, a lot of clover is eaten in the winter; we are also aware that the town birds will gladly come close to be fed with bread! Only the pigeons that are not familiar with bread may refuse to eat it, even when they are hungry (when in doubt, leave it out!) But if these doubting birds see their companions eating bread, they just might give it a go!

It is interesting to note that wood pigeons do not forage only on the ground but also in trees and shrubs, sometimes climbing among extremely thin twigs; quite extraordinary when you consider the size of their plump bodies! They climb very carefully among such twigs, but always seem to be able to maintain their balance.

These birds can even hang upside down if necessary and will do so quite often in order to reach a tasty morsel, especially when berries are ripe.

Care and Breeding: Wild examples of this species are generally difficult to breed, even in a large aviary. Hand-reared specimens or specimens reared by foster parents, however, usually are more accommodating. In my experience, wild examples never lose their shyness, remain exceedingly nervous, and quickly panic at the slightest disturbance. They can thus injure themselves very easily. It is best always to use aviary-bred or aviary-reared birds if you can. Domesticated pigeons, or stock pigeons of a similar size to wood pigeons are the best foster parents. The young should be given water-soaked bread, soft fruits, mealworms and other insects, as well as the normal seed mixtures. Experience has shown that young pigeons reared on seeds alone are likely to contract intestinal problems and die within five days.

Hybrids of wood pigeons with stock pigeons are infertile—not surprising, since wood pigeons are anatomically quite different. Wood pigeons are ornithologically classified as tree pigeons and can, for example, grip narrow twigs with their toes, something that stock doves cannot do.

Speckled Pigeon (*Columba guinea*) (2 subspecies)

Characteristics: Similar in length to the wood pigeon, this species has, however, a more slimly built body. Both sexes are similar in color, and they can usually be distinguished only during the courtship ceremony. The head is gray-blue. The throat and breast are bedecked with lance-shaped, gray-tipped, light cinnamon-colored feathers. The upper back and wing coverts are wine-red, while the median wing coverts have v-shaped white tips. The greater wing coverts are gray, edged with white. The primaries are dark grayish-brown; the insides of the secondaries are wine-red. The rest of the body is deep gray-blue. The beak is black, the cere light gray. There is a naked stripe from the beak to behind the eye. The iris is dark brown; the feet are pale pink. Length: 16⅛ inches (41 cm); weight: 8¾ ounces (250 g).

Natural Range and Behavior: West Africa (Senegal) and deep into East Africa; in the west to north Ghana, and in the east well into south Tanzania. The South African subspecies (from the Cape to southern Angola and Zimbabwe), *C. g. phaenota,* is smaller in build, darker in color, and has smaller v-shaped feather tips.

Both species occur in a wide variety of habitats. I have observed them in various types of woodland (such as Borassus palm woodland; also deciduous and mixed woodland), but also in granite-strewn rocky areas in the savannahs, and in the parks and gardens of towns and settlements. They forage mainly for small fruits and berries, and especially seeds that they pick from the ground. They are fond of peanuts, which should also be offered to captive birds. Wild birds keep in contact with a continual "wourh, wou-wou-wou-wou" call. During courtship, with frequent head bowing, the cock lets out his deep "ourou-cou."

The wide nest is made of twigs and often situated in the crown of a *Borassus* palm. Two eggs are laid and these are incubated for about 16 days. I have also seen nests in rock crevices and even in holes in the walls of village buildings. The young stay in the nest for 20 to 23 days. Out of the breeding season, these pigeons gather in large flocks, sometimes with as many as several hundred individuals.

Care and Breeding: The first breeding successes with this species

The speckled, triangular-spotted, or Guinea pigeon (Columba guinea) is a hardy and easily managed species. It requires a roomy aviary.

occurred in the London Zoo at the turn of the century. Since then, the birds have always been very popular, and with good care can reach a ripe old age. (I know of examples that have lived at least 22 years.) Speckled pigeons like to have a roomy aviary. They will use half-open nest boxes in which to build their twiggy nests (something like a heron's nest). Often, the same nest is used one season after another, after the necessary repairs have been made. Up to three broods a year are the rule rather than the exception!

The speckled pigeon, unfortunately, has a rather bad name for aggressiveness. It should therefore never be kept together with other dove species, unless you have very long aviaries, in which case you can keep several pairs (three or four) together with *Columba livia, Streptopelia roseogrisea "risoria,"* and *Streptopelia decaocto*. The speckled pigeon is cold hardy, but must have access to a dry, draft-free night shelter in the colder months. Food should consist of wheat, corn, milo or sorghum, peanuts, darrum (Indian millet), peas, oats, groats, various kinds of millet, acorns, beechnuts, berries, other small fruits, and a rich variety of greens. A free choice of grit should always be available.

Rameron or Olive Pigeon (*Columba arquatrix*)

Characteristics: Similar in size to the wood pigeon. The forehead, crown, and cheeks are dark wine-red; the throat, sides of the neck, and other parts of the head are paler, and give an impression of lilac. The back feathers and those on the sides of the neck are lance-shaped These are grayish-red with a dark fleck. The upper body and wings are purple reddish-brown, running into gray on the secondaries. The primaries are black, with gray; the tail is black. The breast and belly are

The rameron or olive pigeon (Columba arquatrix) feeds mainly on berries and other fruits. On the wing, this species is a sheer acrobat.

wine-red, covered with white flecks. The beak, orbital ring, legs, and feet are yellow. The iris is gray. Length: 16⅛ inches (41 cm); weight: 10½ to 12⅓ ounces (300 to 350 g).

Natural Range and Behavior: Africa; southern and central Angola, Shaba and Zaire, eastern Zimbabwe to Ethiopia, Natal, and southern and eastern Cape Province. They occur from 3,000 to 10,000 feet (1,000 to 3,200 m) in the mountains, in the crowns of trees, but I have also seen them in juniper woods, which occur at similar altitudes. Knowing the habitat it is logical that these beautiful birds mainly feed on fruits—olives, figs (*Ficus*), fruits of the *Calodendron capense* and from the ironbark tree, *Olea capensis*), and berries (especially those from *Juniperus* and *Podocarpus*). The birds also come regularly to the ground in search of seeds, grit, and the like.

These birds are extremely shy and cautious, in spite of the fact that they frequently occur in towns and villages. Dr. J. Nicolai saw these birds walking on footpaths in the Ngorongoro Crater (Tanzania), and close to the Tree-Tops Hotel near Mount Kenya they pecked up the salt that had been strewn around for the big game animals!

On the wing, rameron pigeons are sheer acrobats. They often fly for miles in search of food, but still return to the same roosting sites in the crowns of the trees each evening. The call is a deep, growling "cou-cou, crou-crou, crou-crou crou-crou" in which the first two syllables uttered are the longest. During the courtship ceremony, the cock flies several meters in the air and dives loudly to the ground in a steep glide. Before reaching the ground he turns and circles above his chosen one, while emitting somewhat bleating sounds. The nests are built in trees and shrubs. The single egg is incubated for 17 days.

Care and Breeding: These colorful and friendly doves need to be kept in an aviary that is roomy and especially tall—10 to 13 feet (3 to 4 m). Breeders have been very successful using such cages with naturally planted trees (such as apple, cherry, and oak). This species is fairly peaceful, and several pairs can be safely kept together. After overcoming their initial shyness, they are soon ready to breed. They first arrived in the London Zoo in 1864 and were first bred in 1912. In addition to a basic dove menu, you can give them a variety of berries, finely chopped fruits, and greens. Peanuts and pinenuts are also appreciated.

My tip: While observing the species in the wild I noticed their eagerness for sorghum, small whole corn, and lentils. Why not spoil your birds once in a while? I do!

Scaly-naped or Puerto Rico Pigeon (*Columba squamosa*)

Characteristics: This beautiful pigeon is similar in size to the rock pigeon, but with a somewhat slimmer body. The head, neck, and throat are wine-red, with a red shimmer on the sides of the neck. The upper body is generally dark slate-gray; the underside notably lighter. The carmine red beak has a paler tip. The orbital ring is orange to scarlet, with a sprinkling of raised yellow papules. The iris is scarlet and the feet are crimson. Length: 6 inches (15 cm); weight: 6½ to 6¾ ounces (185 to 190 g).

Natural Range and Behavior: The Lesser and Greater Antilles, with the exception of Bonaire, Curacao, and Jamaica. This species lives mainly in montane forest, and the birds keep in contact with a loud "wou-wou, hou-hou-hou" call. Nests are constructed in trees and thickly foliaged shrubs, but also occasionally on the ground. The clutch consists of just a single egg.

Care and Breeding: The scaly-naped pigeon was first brought to the London Zoo in 1868, but was not bred until 1876. Since then breeding successes have been regularly reported from many parts of the world. In spite of the availability of nesting platforms and open boxes, they seem to prefer to nest in a hollow on the floor of the aviary.

The small scaled pigeon (Columba speciosa) has neck feathers edged with black. It lives in Central America and northern South America.

Scaled Pigeon (*Columba speciosa*)

Characteristics: The size is similar to the scaly-naped pigeon. The head is purple-brown; the long neck feathers have white tips and purple edges. The upper breast is gold-brown with white streaks; there are copper-colored streaks on the neck. The rest of the breast and the belly is whitish with purple-brown edges to the feathers. The mantle, back, and the rest of the upper body, including the wing coverts, are purple-red; the primaries are black, with narrow white edges.

57

The tail is black, the rump purple-brown. The beak is crimson with a yellow tip; the orbital ring is dark red and surrounded with a blue ring; the iris is purple, and the feet purple-red. Length: 6 inches (15 cm); weight: 6½ ounces (180 g).

Natural Range and Behavior: From southern Mexico to northeastern Argentina. These are inhabitants of the tree canopies, where they forage for a variety of fruits and berries. Sometimes they will let a lot of food drop to the ground, and will later descend to fill their crops. They keep in contact with each other by uttering a loud "hou, hou-hou, hou" call, in which the two middle syllables are faster. The nest is usually constructed high in a tree; the clutch consists of only one egg. Incubation takes 16 to 17 days, and the young leave the nest about 21 days later.

Care and Breeding: The species was imported to the London Zoo in 1868. The first American breeding success can be attributed to the late Prof. C. Naether (California, 1961). Scaled pigeons have remained popu-

lar over the years, in spite of the fact that they are initially shy and can also sit stock-still for hours on a perch or nest platform. Naether's pair started to breed after he had already had them for three years. They used a grass-filled basket that was placed high up in the aviary. This pair was docile and friendly towards its companions and other dove species. Many fanciers keep a single cock with two hens of this species in the aviary. In colder areas, this species must have a warmed winter shelter. As well as fruits and berries, they will take some seeds (especially small grains of corn) and will love some small pieces of cheese.

Picazuro Pigeon (*Columba picazuro*)

Characteristics: Another small species that is mainly slate-gray, with white edges to the wing feathers. The head and underside are light wine-red; a typical neck ring consists of black-edged checkered white or gray feathers. The tail is blue-gray with a black band at the tip. The beak is red, and the skin around the beak is gray with a vague red tinge and a light edge. The iris is pale brown-orange and the feet are dark red. The female is not so brightly colored as the male, and is generally smaller in build. Length: 6 inches (15 cm); weight: 6¾ ounces (190 g).

Natural Range and Behavior: Northeastern Brazil and southwards to the Mato Grosso, and in the provinces of Tucuman and Buenos Aires in Argentina. In the wild this species occurs in forested as well as settled areas. I have observed nesting birds in parks and gardens. During the courtship display, the cock sits as straight as an arrow on a twig and makes rapid head bows and spreads his tail somewhat, while his body remains immobile. After performing

The picazuro pigeon (Columba picazuro) has a neck ring of black-edged feathers. It is distributed throughout Argentina and the southern part of Brazil.

two or three of these maneuvers, he opens his wings and begins to vibrate his whole body, and lets out a loud call. The normal contact call can be described as "ourai-ou-cou, cou-cou-cou." The pair raise only one brood per season. During the winter months this species collects in flocks of 200 or more birds.

Care and Breeding: This really splendid bird was first imported by (again!) the London Zoo in 1868, and was successfully bred in the same year. Today, this species is the most imported dove species in Europe. They are excellent aviary birds, being friendly and easy to breed. They will accept a basket made from twigs or wicker as a nesting platform; this is best wired onto the branches of an aviary shrub. I have personally had success with little platforms with an edge about 1 inch (2.5 cm) attached to the outer wall of the night shelter, and somewhat camouflaged behind a few willow twigs. These birds can be kept out all year, provided they have a damp-proof and draft-proof night shelter that can be slightly warmed in excessively cold periods. In the wild, as well as in captivity, they forage for food on the ground, so it is wise to have a seed hopper near the floor of the aviary. However, I have observed these birds in the wild foraging high in the treetops! The aviary diet consists of wheat, small peas, small corn, small sunflower seeds, finely chopped peanuts, paddy rice, oats, groats, and a variety of berries.

Bronze-naped Pigeon (*Turturoena iriditorques*)

Characteristics: Similar in size to the Barbary dove, this species is slate-gray, with a somewhat darker head. The neck is green with a reddish sheen, and there is a dark yellow to bronze-colored neckband. The rest of the underside is dark wine-red, merg-ing into chestnut brown on the under-tail coverts. The beak is blue-gray with a white tip, the cere is dark red, and the iris is red, pink, grayish-pink or golden yellow. The feet are rose red. The hen is somewhat browner in color, especially on the head and underside. Length: 10½ inches (27 cm); weight: 5½ ounces (155 g).

Natural Range and Behavior: Sierra Leone to northern Angola and Zaire. It is a typical forest dweller and thus shy and reserved in the aviary. The nest is built in a thickly foliaged shrub and the clutch consists of two eggs. The most important forage foods are various berries and other small fruits from trees and taller shrubs. They forage alone or as single pairs.

Care and Breeding: The first specimens arrived at the London Zoo in 1928. In the aviary they are relatively peaceful birds that, unlike their wild cousins, will descend to the floor for food. Basic foods include green peas, whole shelled peanuts, milo, and dar-rum. As far as I know, this species is yet to be bred in captivity.

Mauritius Pink Pigeon (*Nesoenas mayeri*)

Characteristics: A little larger than the rock pigeon. It is mainly soft slate-gray with dark brownish-green wings. The forehead is almost white, and the back light brownish pink. The rump is light gray-blue and the tail chestnut brown. The beak is yellow with a red base. The orbital ring is red, the iris yellow, and the feet rose-red. Length: 6.7 inches (17 cm); weight: 7¾ ounces (220 g).

Natural Range and Behavior: The island of Mauritius, where the birds live mainly in the forests. It is estimated that only 12 to 15 pairs still persist in the wild. It is suspected that introduced monkeys are the main cause of the demise of the pink pigeon as the monkeys steal eggs and/or young

The Mauritius pink pigeon (Nesoenas mayeri) is in great danger! It is estimated that only 10 to 15 pairs still survive in the wild!

from the nests. So near extinction, it is improbable that this species can survive. The birds feed on flowers, leaf-buds, young leaves, a variety of tree fruits, and berries. It is interesting that the birds like the fruits and leaves of the poisonous *Euphorbia pyrifolia,* which makes the meat of the pigeons inedible. According to Dr. Raethel, the nest—a euphemism!—is constructed in 48 hours.

Care and Breeding: The species was first imported to the London Zoo in 1906. The first known captive breeding dates from 1977 (Jersey Wildlife Preservation Trust), but the young were lost to trichonomiasis. Thanks to the mild climate of the English Channel island of Jersey, Mauritius pink pigeons have been successfully bred from the late 1970s, starting in 1978 when four youngsters were raised.

The diet consists of wheat and various millets, together with small fruits, lettuce, germinating niger seed, squash, and chopped boiled egg, all mixed together and supplemented with a good vitamin/mineral preparation. Twigs with blossoms, buds and/or young leaves of hawthorn, whitethorn or may (*Crataegus monogyna*), and tortured willow, (*Salix matsudana*), are also given.

Genus *Streptopelia*

This genus contains various well-known species of turtledoves, which are easy to distinguish from the foregoing genera by their medium size. Some members of the genus possess conspicuous checkered neck markings.

Turtledoves are found mainly in rather difficult to reach and somewhat deserted parts of the temperate and tropical parts of Europe, Asia, and Africa. Some species have been successfully introduced to Australia, New Zealand, and the Pacific Islands. Care and breeding of most of the species in aviaries (including small aviaries) pose few problems. They are thus highly recommended for beginners to gain experience before turning to more "difficult" species.

Turtledove (*Streptopelia turtur*) (4 subspecies)

(Other names: European Turtledove, Common Turtledove)

Characteristics: Very similar to the Barbary dove, perceptibly smaller than the wood pigeon, and differing from the collared dove mainly by the black-white patch on the sides of the neck; the collared dove has the characteristic, white-edged, black, half-moon shaped neck patch. The top of the head and the neck are blue-gray, the back and the wing coverts are rusty brown, with many black streaks in the middle of the feathers; the primary flight feathers and the strikingly long tail are both dark brown. The end of the tail is broadly edged with white. The chin, the sides of the head, and the throat have a fine wine-colored glow; the remainder of the underside is dirty white. The iris is golden, yellow, or light orange. The orbital-ring is dark reddish-purple, the beak is black with a purple tinge, and the feet are purplish-red. The hen is sometimes more brightly colored than the cock, but is normally duller and paler. Juvenile birds are similar to their parents except that the crown, sides of the head, and neck are brown and there are no black and white markings on the neck. The whole plumage is somewhat less glossy. Length: 10.6 inches (27 cm); weight: 5⅝ ounces (160 g).

The turtledove has a reputation for its strong and dexterous flying powers, but even outside the courtship period it never flies in a straight line. In fact, the flight is jerky and bumpy, almost as though it is a struggle for the bird to keep in the air. On the ground, however, the dove is quick, nimble, and elegant. During migrations, the birds fly in "confused" groups, in pairs, or even singly. The turtledove migrates from the Mediterranean lands to tropical Africa, where it spends the winter.

Members of the North African strain (*S. t. arenicola*) (which also occur on the Balearic Islands) are lighter in color than the European nominate strain (*S. t. turtur*), which breeds in Europe and western Asia. The eastern populations have the same scientific name, but are conspicuously smaller and paler, especially those from Asia Minor to Iran. *S. t. hoggara* from the central Sahara and the oases at Fezzan and Tibesti, and *S. t. isabellus* from the Dakla Oasis, the Nile Delta, and Fayum are richer in color.

Natural Range and Behavior: Very abundant in England, this species ranges throughout Europe to Madeira, the Canary Islands, North Africa, the oases in the Sahara, western and southern Asia. It is gradually increasing its range in Europe, and in Holland, Belgium, Denmark, and England, for example, it occurs in heathland, woodland, duneland, plantations, cultivated land, gardens, and parks—even in peat bogs! Like the collared dove, this species can be a pest in grain stores and mills, where they occur in great numbers and are frequently poisoned—a method that leaves much to be desired!

The flat nest of this species is a fragile and untidy pretext made of sticks and twigs. If you look up at the nest from below, you can often see the eggs! Eggs are often lost because of the inefficiency of the nest. The nest is constructed in trees, shrubs, and hedges; hawthorn is particularly favored, and occasionally conifers. The nest is usually situated close to the ground and usually close to the trunk. Sometimes several nests are constructed close together, especially

The turtledove (Streptopelia turtur) is a common inhabitant of wooded country in Europe, and in a large part of western Asia and northern Africa, but not as widespread as the laughing dove.

In spring the turtledove's purring call can be heard from tree tops and bushes, usually in the vicinity of water.

in areas where nesting opportunities are scarce, as in open terrain with few trees. Both sexes construct the nest. The breeding season starts in mid-May to June for the first brood and in July to August for the second. Very occasionally a third brood will be reared. The clutch consists of two, rarely three eggs; if there are more eggs than that in the nest, they must have come from two hens. Both sexes share in the incubation of the glossy, white-shelled eggs (30.7 mm × 23.0 mm), which hatch in 13 to 14 days. The young fledge at about 14 days old, when conditions and food are good, but it can take as long as three weeks. Should a predator come close to the nest, the adult birds will try and attract its attention away with wild and loud wing beatings.

During courtship the cock bows very frequently and rapidly, especially as he approaches the hen and looks her "in the face." He then stretches himself up and spreads his neck feathers so that he appears to have a black and silver collar. In the display flight he flies jerkily into the air and glides down with wings and tail spread. Before actual copulation, the birds walk around and peck themselves behind the wings. Mainly the cocks do this but sometimes the hens do also. Sometimes they try a bit of "fencing" with their beaks, the cock being more aggressive in this respect than the hen. A few sham fights result in the hen's taking a more defensive posture. Directly after copulation, the cock stands upright, just like a penguin, but with spread neck feathers, while the hen runs around him as if on parade.

The turtledove is well-known for its long "toourr-tourr-tourr-rourr" call, which is performed with the beak closed. In fact, the word "turtle" in the name is derived from the call. The hen calls less frequently than the cock, and her call is also softer and less musical in tone. A bird in danger can let out a fairly convincing alarm call. When excited, this species can make a sound resembling a cork popping out of a bottle. The call is uttered very quickly during the courtship dance.

Turtledoves forage for food on the ground, pulling seeds from the heads of grasses, etc. Seeds of broad-leaved plants are also eaten, especially Fumaria (fumitory), plus all kinds of grains, buds, leaves, small slugs, and other invertebrates.

Care and Breeding: As we see frequently, captive-born and reared birds breed much more readily and easily than wild-caught specimens; which can stay shy and nervous for years. If you have a large aviary you can keep several pairs of turtledoves together (one pair, three pairs, or more, but never two pairs). Nest platforms, 8 × 8 inches; (20 × 20 cm) with a 1-inch (2.5 cm) high edge, can be installed as high as possible on the inner wall of the night shelter. Although you can obtain commercial seed mixtures for turtledoves, they will also thrive on a good budgerigar mix, plus a little hemp, wheat, milo, and canary seed. A rich variety of greens must, of course, be included. With proper care, these charming and popular doves will reach a ripe old age; Dr. Raethel gives examples of 22 and 34 years.

According to Dr. Jean Delacour, hybrids of Barbary doves and turtledoves are fertile. During the winter months, the birds should be kept in a slightly warmed shelter. For further information, see Barbary dove (page 65).

Collared Dove, or Indian Ring-necked Dove (*Streptopelia decaocto*) (*3 subspecies*)

(Other names: Collared Turtledove, Ring Dove, Eastern Ring Dove, and European Ring Dove).

Characteristics: This well-known and often kept dove is somewhat larger than the Barbary dove. In 1955, this species bred in the wild in England for the first time and has since increased its range tremendously; in fewer than ten years the English population of doves increased to more than 20,000 birds, and the species has also spread throughout northwestern Europe.

The collared dove is about the same size as the previous species, but has a longer tail. It is uniformly grayish-yellow above, while the underside is gray with a soft, pinkish tinge. Very obvious distinguishing features from the turtledove are the black, half-moon-shaped neck marking, and the gray under-tail coverts and, particularly, the different call. In flight, the difference can be seen especially on the underside of the spread tail; the tail marking of the turtledove is a wide, white, end-border, broken exactly in the center with a black stripe, while in the collared dove, the white border is complete, without the black stripe. Length: 11 inches (28 cm); weight: 6⅓ to 8¾ ounces (180 to 250 g).

The collared dove (Streptopelia decaocto) is found only in the close vicinity of human habitations in parks and gardens. It nests in trees and shrubs, but also on roofs and the eaves of buildings.

The pink-headed dove (Streptopelia roseogrisea) of central Africa is the creamy-brown "ancestor" of the well-known Barbary dove. The nominate form may very well be a geographical race of the collared dove, which has a gray-brown plumage.

The color pattern described here is for the nominate form, *S. d. decaocto,* which occurs in India, the Middle East, Europe, China, and Korea. The subspecies *S. d. stoliczcae* from Chinese Turkestan is larger in build and generally paler in color; *S. d. xanthocyl,* from the Irrawaddy Delta in Burma is darker, and has an intense yellow orbital ring (instead of white).

Natural Range and Behavior: This charming bird has a very wide range, including most of continental Europe, through to the Middle East, southern Israel, and eastward to India. Year after year its range is gradually increasing, as it makes inroads into eastern Saudi Arabia, Chinese Turkestan, northern, central, and western China, Korea, and even parts of Japan. In India, Sri Lanka, Burma, and other parts of Asia, the collared dove is to be found in wooded areas as well as in cultivated areas. In the other areas named above the birds are to be found closer to residential areas, even in towns and villages, sometimes in large numbers. It is assumed that the collared dove made

its way into northern China, Korea, and Japan via India.

Collared doves nest in trees and shrubs, but sometimes also on roofs and the like. As with the preceding species, the nest is an untidy bundle of twigs, and the eggs can often be seen through the structure from below. Both sexes construct the nest. The breeding season can run from mid-February to September/October. The hen usually lays two (rarely three) glossy white eggs (31.9×24.0 mm). There are three or four broods per season. The incubation time is 14 to 16 days and the young leave the nest 15 to 17 days after hatching. They sometimes return to the nest at night to roost for a few days thereafter.

The courtship display is similar to that of the Barbary dove (*Streptopelia "risoria"*) (see page 65). The collared dove is a very popular cage and aviary dove. The cock begins with a bowing ceremony, whereby the beak nearly touches the ground. The neck feathers are fluffed out to form a collar, the tail is spread like a fan, and the wings are usually flapping and clapping. At the same time the bird moves in half circles before the hen. In the display flight, the cock flies high in the air and claps the wings before gliding to earth, often in a spiral, with outstretched wings and fanned tail.

The collared dove, has a very characteristic call that is repeated frequently as if the bird is trying to see how long it can keep it up. The call is something like "gour-grour-gour." The call is also used when the birds are at the nest, but is then somewhat quieter and more stretched out. During pairing the sound uttered is more like "gou-gou-gou," the last note being short and soft.

When excited, the birds utter a nasal call that is similar to the harsh mating cry of the peacock. During flight and landing the same nasal cry can be heard: "che-che-che-che."

The wild ancestor of the domesticated and popular Barbary dove comes from North Africa.

The main food consists of seeds foraged on the ground. In many areas, the collared dove has become a culture follower and lives well from the kindness of people. Especially during the difficult winter months, bread and potato crumbs are eagerly devoured, as are all kinds of berrries and seeds. The birds most probably also take slugs and other small invertebrates.

Care and Breeding: Collared doves were first successfully bred in the United States. Wild specimens, as with most species, pose some difficulties when brought into captivity; but hand-reared, or aviary-bred birds are quite tame and charming. There is no difficulty with fostering, especially if Barbary doves are used as foster parents. Although collared doves are quite hardy, I still think it best to keep them in a slightly warmed winter shelter—or at least one free from cold

winds and dampness—to avoid the possibility of frostbite of the toes, to which collared doves are susceptible.

Hybrids with the Barbary dove are fertile in both sexes, and in the F1-generation (birds of Dr. J. Nicolai), they use the calls of both parents. Hybrid collared dove × Barbary dove have a three-syllable courtship call, like that of the father but with a rolling "r" and a slightly different pitch. Hybrid Barbary dove × collared dove (also according to Dr. Nicolai), have a two-syllable call, without the rolling "r" of the Barbary dove.

Barbary Dove (*Streptopelia roseogrisea* var. *"risoria"*)

Characteristics: Somewhat smaller than the collared dove, it is mainly grayish-yellow with a black neck band. The outer wing coverts and primaries are brown. The rump and center tail feathers (the latter with white tips) are also grayish-yellow. The beak is black, the iris red, the feet carmine-red. Length: 5 inches (13 cm); weight: 4 ounces (115 g).

Natural Range and Behavior: The wild ancestor of the domesticated Barbary dove comes from the savannah regions of North Africa, south of the Sahara, along the coast of Sudan and Somalia, and into central and southern Saudi Arabia. It is difficult to say when and where this dove was domesticated, but Saudia Arabia or the East Indies is a good guess. At present, these extremely popular birds are bred in most parts of the world, and will even breed well in cages, though I personally consider this kind of accommodation far from ideal. I prefer to see them in a roomy garden aviary. In the United States, the Barbary dove is much used experimentally in behavioral and endocrinological studies.

Care and Breeding: I have frequently seen these birds raise one brood after another in cages! In a gar-

The spotted, Chinese-necklaced, pearl-necked, or spotted Chinese turtledove (Streptopelia chinensis) is very common in its natural range and is easily managed in captivity.

den aviary several pairs (but never two pairs, always one pair or three or more pairs) can be kept together in community with, for example, finches, small parakeets, and pheasants. The birds must be kept in slightly warmed quarters in the winter. As foster parents they are, in one word, outstanding! They are especially useful in the rearing of bleeding-heart pigeons and other costly and difficult-to-breed species. Once you get your Barbary doves accustomed to feeding on ant pupae, small, living mealworms, egg food, and a commercial rearing food for canaries, they will have no problems with rearing those difficult species. As soon as the young are independent, the foster parents can be put back on their seed diet consisting of millet varieties, canary seed, hemp, milo, and wheat, plus greens and a calcium supplement.

At breeding time you can give them some small nesting platforms or—indoors—cardboard boxes in which you have laid some straw and hay. The hen lays two eggs that are incubated for 14 to 15 days. The young fledge at 14 to 15 days, but are usually still fairly helpless, often sitting in a corner of the aviary floor (where they could become victims of other aggressive aviary inmates, especially if the aviary is not very large). After about a month, the parents stop feeding their young or foster young and begin with a new clutch. Six clutches a year are not unusual! According to Dr. Raethel, a Barbary dove in England lived in captivity for 23 years.

Various mutations have been cultured over the years.

Spotted Dove (*Streptopelia chinensis*) (4 subspecies)
(Other names: Pearl-necked Dove, and Chinese Turtledove)

Characteristics: Somewhat smaller, and with shorter wings and a longer tail than the collared dove. Two of the subspecies (*S. c. chinensis* and *S. c. suratensis*) are regularly available. The *chinensis,* from southern China, has a slate-gray head; the other subspecies is characterized by its smaller size and paler coloring. The "pearled" neck marking (black feathers with white spots) is a striking characteristic. The top of the back, the wing coverts, and the inner parts of the primaries are wine-red; the neck, breast, and belly, however, are light red. The other upper parts are various shades of gray. The beak is black, the iris is brown , and the feet are dark red. The *suratensis* is paler in color, and with black-tipped white undertail coverts. The "pearled" neck marking has red patches. Length: 5 inches (13 cm); weight: 4 ounces (115 g).

Natural Range and Behavior: India, Sri Lanka, southern China, Indochina, and the Malay-Indonesian Archipelago; colonized successfully into Hawaii, California, and eastern Australia. The birds live mainly in wooded areas, but also in cultivated land, parks, and gardens. The typical call is "houch-cou-cou ou ou." The hen lays two eggs that are incubated for 14 to 16 days. The young leave the nest after about 15 days.

Care and Breeding: First imported into Amsterdam (Artis Zoo) in 1843; where the subspecies *suratensis* also first arrived in 1951. The birds are naturally shy; they breed easily, but need adequate space so that they have room for flight, if necessary. In small aviaries they will stay wild and nervous for a long time, and are aggressive towards their own kind. I always think it better to give each pair an aviary to itself as during the breeding season they can become quite pugnacious. In winter, they are best kept in a slightly warmed shelter. They require a typical dove diet of various millets, canary seed, a little hemp, dari, milo, and a rich variety of greens.

Laughing Dove (*Streptopelia senegalensis*) (5 subspecies)

(Other names: Senegal Dove and Palm Dove)

Characteristics: Smaller than the Barbary dove, the cock has a splendid red-brown head, throat, and breast. The throat band is black with dark reddish-brown flecks. The back is reddish-brown with a gray sheen; the underside and the chin are white. The eyes are brown, with a red orbital ring. The beak is black, and the feet red-brown to red. The female is mainly gray. Length: about 4.6 inches (12 cm); weight: 3⅛ to 4¼ ounces (90 to 120 g).

Natural Range and Behavior: Africa, Saudi Arabia, Turkestan, and Afghanistan. Probably introduced in Turkey, Israel, Syria, and Malta. Successful colonies in and around Perth, Australia. The birds live in open, dry terrain, but also occur near villages and settlements, parks, etc. Their flight is very noisy. The call is a weak "ou ou-ou ou." In fact these birds are relatively quiet. They build their nests fairly large (in relation to their size) in thick creepers.

The laughing, Senegal or palm dove (Streptopelia senegalensis) is widespread throughout Africa, south and central Asia, and India. It is an inexpensive, hardy species.

67

Care and Breeding: These doves are quiet and sociable and are quite suited to a roomy community aviary, but will quarrel with other doves. Their care is similar to that described for the diamond dove (see page 81) but they will also eat insects. You should also have a conifer or two planted in the aviary, as they seem to prefer these for nesting. The nest is much more substantial than that of other species. To avoid accidental loss of eggs or young, it is best to place nesting platforms of wire mesh or wood among the twigs, or to place a wooden plank under the nest after it has been built. Both parents incubate, and the young hatch in two weeks. Remarkably, the cock feeds the hen when she is incubating, but never the reverse! The young leave the nest at about 12 days old, but are fed by the parents for about 10 days thereafter. Once independent, the young must be separated from the adults, as the latter will want to start another brood and can get very aggressive towards their older offspring, sometimes with very unpleasant results! They are very fertile birds that can easily raise 6 broods per season if their aviary is in a light and sunny situation (wild birds can produce eight or more broods per season).

Laughing doves quickly become tame and often will not move even during a nest inspection. The birds should be kept in slightly warmed or frost-free indoor accommodations during the winter.

My tip: I like to provide my birds with old thrush nests and flower pots partly filled with mulch—with great success!

The subspecies *S. s. cambayensis,* from Asia, can be distinguished by its plain gray upper parts; this bird is often sold as "laughing dove" in the trade, and usually no distinction of the subspecies is made.

The nominate form was first imported by the London Zoo in 1861, the *cambayensis* subspecies some 40 years later. Both strains are usually peaceful and quiet, but quarrels can arise in the breeding season among themselves and with other small dove species. The first white mutations appeared in Russia during 1962; in 1977 the first pied mutations appeared in South Africa. Feed them on a rich variety of greens, plus various millet varieties, canary seed, milo, dari, and a good budgerigar mixture.

Genera *Turtur, Tympanistria, Chalcopelia, and Oena*

The African doves in these genera are about the size of the diamond dove and are very popular in the aviary, mainly beause they are willing breeders. They are generally roundish in build, with a short tail, but a notable exception is the Cape dove that has a slender body and a long tail. The glossy plumage of the shoulders and wings is striking, as is the reddish-brown inside of the primaries. The Cape dove lives mainly in savannah grasslands, but I have seen them close to settlements and even in parks; all of the other species live mainly in wooded areas, but do not necessarily avoid human habitations.

Green-spotted Wood Dove (*Turtur chalcospilos*) (3 subspecies)

Characteristics: About one-third smaller than the Barbary dove, and similar in appearance to the blue-spotted wood dove (*Turtur afer*), but lighter in color. It has a gray head with black eyebrow stripe. The neck and the underside are wine-red. The throat is white, as are the undertail coverts. The back is light reddish-brown. There are two black crossbands separated by a yellowish-brown border on the lowest part of the back. The tail is bluish-gray, and the outer tail feathers have white edges and black tips. There are two glossy-green to blue-green wing patches. The beak is black, red at the base; the iris is brown, and the feet dark red. Length: 4 inches (10 cm); weight: 3⅝ ounces (100 g).

Natural Range and Behavior: Ethiopia to the northern part of southwest Africa; also in Transvaal, Natal, and eastern Capeland. This species inhabits dry woodlands, but in the vicinity of water (creeks, rivers, lakes). They forage for seeds, snails, and insects in open areas. The call has a melancholy lilt. The nest is a flimsy affair, constructed about 12 feet (4 m) high in a tree. The hen lays two eggs that are incubated for 13 days. The young leave the nest after 13 days, but are weak at first and sit on the ground; three days later they can take to the wing.

Care and Breeding: These interesting, vivacious, and colorful birds first arrived in the London Zoo in 1866 and were successfully bred there in the same year. Since then they have been readily available in the trade. They seem to thrive best in a large aviary, where they can potter about on the floor, taking cover in thick shrubbery if alarmed. It is thus important to have some thick growing plants in the flight. It is well-known that members of this species are "sun worshippers" and will always bask in a sunny part of the aviary. They breed well, and 3 to 4 broods per year are not exceptional. The diet should consist of various varieties of millet, some hemp (in fall and winter), a good canary or budgerigar rearing food, small insects (ant pupae, mealworms, and especially snails) and greens. They must be kept in a warm spot during the winter.

Blue-spotted Wood Dove
(*Turtur afer*) (2 subspecies)

Characteristics: Similar in size and appearance to the preceding species,

hence somewhat smaller than the Barbary dove. The cock has a gray head with a conspicuous white forehead and light red cheeks. The wings and back are brownish-gray; the wings have dark purplish flecks and the feathers are edged in black. The throat and breast are red; the rest of the lower body is white. The iris is brown, the beak is black, and the feet are rose-red. The hen is less sharply patterned, duller in color, and is somewhat smaller. Length: about 8 inches (20 cm); weight: 4 ounces (115 g).

Natural Range and Behavior: Africa from Ethiopia and Senegal to Angola and northeastern Transvaal. They live in wooded country but never far from water. The call and the breeding habits are similar to the preceding species.

Care and Breeding: This species is not very tolerant towards its own or other dove species. But the bird is frequently available commercially. They nest relatively close to the ground, preferably in thick foliage; two broods per season is quite normal. Their hardiness and readiness to breed make them well worth keeping. General care

The female tambourine dove differs from the male in having white parts suffused with gray.

The tambourine dove (Turtur tympanistria) is a popular species. It needs a somewhat secluded aviary with natural cover.

is similar to that described for the diamond dove (see page 81). After two weeks of incubation by both cock and hen the young (usually two) hatch from the eggs. As soon as they are independent, the young must be separated from the parents. It is recommended that strong nesting platforms be provided, as the nest itself is very flimsy. During the breeding season, the birds should be offered insects as a supplement to the normal dove diet.

There is a subspecies, *T. a. kilimensis,* that has a wholly red beak. This bird is also usually available on the market and requires similar care to the nominate race.

T. afer afer was first exhibited in the Amsterdam Zoo (Artis) during 1872; the first successful breeding took place in the Jardin d'Acclimation in Paris. This easy-to-breed species is especially suitable for beginners to the fancy as it will tolerate regular nest

inspections, though I like to keep these to a minimum, or none, when all seems to be going well. The birds should be placed in slightly warmed winter accommodation.

Tambourine Dove (*Tympanistria [Turtur] tympanistria*) (3 subspecies)

Characteristics: About ⅓ smaller than the Barbary dove. The first primary wing feather is typically sharply tipped. The cock is mainly white (the hen gray), with dark brown undertail coverts and central tail feathers; the rest of the tail feathers are gray with black cross barring. There is a black eyebrow stripe. The upper parts are dark brown with, an olive-green sheen, running into a gray sheen at the neck. The lowest part of the back has two black and one lighter crossband. The wings are olive-green, with glossy bluish-green highlights; in the hen these are smaller. The beak is red, the iris dark brown and the feet are purple-red. Length: 4 inches (10 cm); weight: 3⅞ ounces (110 g).

Natural Range and Behavior: Africa, from Sierra Leone and southern Ethiopia to Angola, Natal, and Cape Province. These charming, nimble birds inhabit wooded areas, not too far from water, where they forage much on the ground in the open glades for berries, seeds, and insects. The nest is just a flimsy platform. The hen lays two eggs that hatch in 13 days. The young leave the nest about 14 days later and are fully independent in another seven days. Already at eight weeks the first white marking appears on the head.

Care and Breeding: This species was first imported by the London Zoo in 1871, but the first breeding results were not reported until 1903 (A. G. Butler, England). It is unfortunately imported irregularly and only in small numbers; the birds remain shy at first and disappear into the shrubbery at the slightest disturbance. They never really become tame. During the breeding season the cocks can get aggressive towards their own or other dove species, so a single pair per aviary is recommended. Like the green-spotted wood dove, the tambourine dove also is fond of sun basking, so the aviary should have a few sunny spots. Some dishes of dry river sand will be used by the doves for sand bathing. Nesting platforms of wire mesh should be placed in thick foliage and covered with the beech leaves and thuja twigs upon which the birds will build their nest.

My tip: I never dispose of old nests built by laughing doves, as tambourine doves like to use them for their own family!

The young open their eyes at five days, and the first primary feather appears after 35 days. It is amusing to see how quickly the young can peck up ant pupae. In addition to millet, rearing food, and insects, oily seeds (*Ricinus*) and hemp (through the year) are essential. Small sunflower seeds, chopped peanuts and pine nuts, and berries are also important.

Cape Dove (*Oena capensis*) (2 subspecies)

(Other names: Masked Dove and Namaqua Dove)

Characteristics: A little larger than the diamond dove. The cock is mainly black; black tail, black mask (the hen does not have a black mask), black throat, and black breast. The shoulders, the neck and the crown are dark gray; the mantle is brown. The sides of the neck, the lower breast, and the belly are white. There is a darker form on Madagascar. The eyes are brown; the beak and feet are purplish-red. Length: 9 inches (22 cm); weight: 1⅜ ounces (40 g).

Natural Range and Behavior: Along the Red Sea to deep into south-

western Saudi Arabia and Southern Africa; further, in Senegal and the Sudan. They prefer dry, open terrain, but are to be seen in villages and cultivated areas in small family groups. They are very acrobatic in flight and spread the tail widely like a fan when coming in to land.

Care and Breeding: This is an attractive little dove that is usually quite easy to obtain. It is a fairly easy species to keep—even in a large community aviary, where it will not interfere with other birds.

Cape doves quickly become tame and learn to accept treats from the fancier's hand. With care as described for the diamond dove (see page 81), the birds will thrive. Wooden, or wire-mesh nesting platforms should be provided. In the wild, the doves construct a nest from small roots and grass in thick foliage. The hen lays two cream-

The cape, masked or Namaqua dove (Oena capensis) is somewhat delicate in cold climates. A well-lit night shelter is essential.

In courtship, the male Cape dove lowers his head, raises his tail, and, with vibrating wings, gives a cooing call.

colored eggs. The incubation time is two weeks and the young leave the nest at 16 to 18 days of age. Several broods per season are not unusual.

This species was first imported by the Amsterdam Zoo (Artis) in 1854, while the first breeding success occurred in Germany (by von Wartenburg) in 1875. It is fairly intolerant of cold and damp, so must be brought indoors during the winter. It must have facilities to sun bask in its outdoor aviary. Sometimes a pair takes several years before it starts to breed. Give the birds a basket or platform fixed into the foliage of a shrub. Many pairs are ready to start on a new brood before they have reared the existing one, and abandon the young. Diamond doves make good foster parents in such cases. Food includes various millets, canary seed, canary mixture, greens, and vitamin/mineral supplements.

Genera *Chalcophaps, Phaps, Ocyphaps, Petrophassa,* and *Leucosarcia*

These genera are characterized by short-tailed, compact birds with fairly long legs, and conspicuous metallic markings on the wings and sometimes the back. Particular exceptions are two species that are commonly seen in the fancy: first, the crested pigeon, that is typified mainly by the pattern of black, blue-gray, white, and red on the face; and second, the wonga pigeon (see page 80).

Emerald Dove (*Chalcophaps indica*) (9 subspecies)

Characteristics: Similar in size to the Barbary dove. The nominate form has a white forehead and a white stripe above the eye; the hen has only the white forehead. The crown and neck of the cock are gray, the throat and breast, wine-red. This red merges grad-

The emerald dove flies at great speed through and around trees and shrubs, so it will need a spacious aviary.

ually into gray down the sides and into the belly. The white shoulder patch is a very typical characteristic in the cock, but absent in the hen. The upper back and wings are a metallic greenish-copper color. The rump and upper tail coverts are gray. The middle tail feathers are dark brown, while the outer feathers are gray with black edges. The beak, the feet, and the orbital ring are coral-red; the iris is brown-red. Dr. Raethel reported a blue mutation, but unfortunately I have no further details. Length: 5 inches (13 cm); weight: 2½ to 3⅞ ounces (70 to 110 g).

My tip: In the wild this species avoid close contact with turtledoves. Therefore, I never have the two species in the same aviary. Emerald doves do, however, tolerate laughing doves.

Natural Range and Behavior: This abundant species, with its several geographical strains, occurs in southern Asia, northern and eastern Australia, southeastern New Guinea, the Philippines, the Sunda Islands, Hainan, Assam, and northern India.

All of the strains range through woodland, grassland, and mountainous areas. They forage for food on the ground, especially in woodland glades, but I have also seen them close to

The female of the emerald dove (Chalcophaps indica) lacks the white eyebrow. The species is an excellent aviary bird; it likes to roost high.

human habitations, near to houses and on footpaths. They eat many seeds, berries, and termites. The call of this species can be irritating, as it utters a nasal "hou-oun-hou-oun-hou-oun" for hours on end. It is recognized as an exceptional acrobat.

Care and Breeding: The nominate form was first brought to England in 1795 (Osterley Park Menagerie). Dr. Karl Russ first bred it in Berlin in 1880. This species often does not recognize the aviary mesh as an obstacle, with the result that it can fly at full speed into it. Serious injuries and fatalities result. I have usually been able to prevent such occurrences by planting shrubs close to the mesh (inside or out) and threading twigs with foliage through the mesh (especially in the breeding season). These birds fly at great speed through and around the trees and shrubs in the wild, so will, of course, need a spacious aviary. The best form of planting is foliage trees or shrubs with many horizontal branches that are used as perches (oak and fruit trees, for example). During late fall and winter, the birds should be kept in slightly warmed indoor accommoda-tions. Here, horizontal branches must also be available; the birds have an interesting habit of walking along branches, even small twigs, length-wise. I personally find these to be excellent aviary birds that are quite tolerant towards other dove species. A nesting basket, on which they will build a large nest, should be affixed high in the aviary. The incubation time is two weeks, and the young stay in the nest for a similar time, occasionally two or three days less. The courtship display of the cock, with the beak pressed against his breast and the wings spread out, is exceptionally interesting. It can happen that the cock will get aggressive towards other birds during the breeding season, but this is rare if the aviary is large enough. A good budgerigar seed mixture makes a basis for the diet, although emerald doves are also fond of oily seeds such as hemp, crushed sunflower seeds, crushed peanuts, and oats. A good canary rearing food, a variety of berries and insects (mealworms, ant pupae, etc.) are also important. Throughout the year, but especially in the breeding season, the birds should additionally be given a regular vitamin/mineral supplement to avoid complications with bone growth and similar deficiency problems (especially in the growing young).

The bronze-winged pigeon (Phaps chalcoptera) prefers open bushland. In captivity, the various seeds should be offered in separate dishes.

Bronze-winged Pigeon (*Phaps chalcoptera*) (3 subspecies)

(Other names: Common Bronzewing, Forest Bronzewing)

Characteristics: Similar in size to the wood pigeon. The sexes are difficult to distinguish from each other. The cock has a white forehead; the crown is brown, and this is also reflected on the forehead. The sides of the head are glossy purple with a reddish sheen. It has a conspicuous black bridle. Other parts of the head and neck are whitish gray, with a thin white stripe over the eye and cheek. The throat is light white. The back is brown with a gray undersheen and lighter edges to the feathers. The belly is red, merging into reddish gray near the tail. The wing is brown and gray with a conspicuous bronze-colored and a blue-gray-green patch. The eyes are reddish-brown, the beak gray-black, and the feet deep red. The hen is not quite so brightly patterned and colored and her wing patches are yellowish-green. The forehead is gray. Length: 13¾ inches (35 cm); weight: 17⅝ ounces (500 g).

Natural Range and Behavior: Australia, including Tasmania. It does not occur in the rain forests of northern Queensland and prefers open bush land where it spends most of its time on the ground. The flight is quite rapid. It rarely goes to drink during the day, only at dawn or dusk. After the first juvenile molt, the yellow feathers of the hen are replaced by gray ones.

Care and Breeding: This ground-loving dove has recently been kept and bred quite extensively. Bronzewings seem to do best as a single pair in a large aviary. The cock gets extremely aggressive during the breeding season. Otherwise they are generally good breeders, if provided with a simple open nest-box fixed not too high in a thickly foliaged shrub. Two or three broods per year is quite normal. These birds live almost exclusively on starchy seeds (wheat, etc.), acacia seeds, and, in the wild, even the poisonous seeds of heart-leaf poison pea, *Gastrolobium bilobum.* With good care, the young quickly become tame and trusting and will breed readily. They can breed at a fair age to about 15 years!

It is a good idea to affix a long perching plank high in the aviary (see crested pigeon, page 76). The dry aviary floor may be partly covered with a layer of pine needles. I would avoid nest inspections. Pairing takes place on the ground. As juveniles are sus-

The brush bronze-wing (Phaps elegans) lives mainly in coastal areas. In captivity, pairs should be kept separately to avoid fighting.

ceptible to rachitis, give supplementary food in the form of germinated millet with (cod) liver oil, adequate greens, and calcium. The normal menu consists of various millets (especially silver millet), canary seed, oats, hemp, poppy seed, and the like. The food should be offered in open dishes. In the fall, berries are always a welcome addition to the diet. Commercial egg food will also not be refused, especially during the breeding period.

During the winter these birds should be placed in a warm room, as they are susceptible to frozen toes. They can live for 20 years or more.

Brush Bronzewing (*Phaps elegans*)
(Other name: Little Bronze Pigeon)
Characteristics: Shorter than the preceding species, but plumper, and with shorter wings and tail. The cock is mainly gray; only the forehead is grayish yellow-brown. It has a brown neck band. The cheeks are white, as is the area around the eye. The neck and back are brownish, The shoulders and underside are greenish-gray. There is a chestnut-brown patch on the throat. There is a

The Australian flock pigeon (Phaps histri-onica) has become very scarce, with small flocks occuring only in the north.

yellowish sheen to the gray wing feathers. The eyes are brown, the beak is gray-black, and the feet are dark purplish-red. The hen is less sharply colored and patterned. Length: 12.6 inches (32 cm); weight: 17⅝ ounces (500 g).

Natural Range and Behavior: Southwestern and southeastern Australia and Tasmania. Lives mainly in marsh and thick bush land, especially in coastal areas.

The active crested pigeon (Ocyphaps lophotes) doesn't thrive very well in wet and cold conditions.

Care and Breeding: This close relation of the preceding species is also widely kept by fanciers and does especially well in large flights planted with low shrubs and grass. Though not such a ready breeder as the foregoing species, success is not out of the question. The fancier should provide a "helping hand." I have had best results with pairs kept in separate aviaries—in consideration of the often aggressive behavior of the cock. The hen lays two eggs in an almost "see-through" nest that is constructed in a shrub close to the ground; therefore provide a choice of wire mesh or wooden nest platforms in such places. Both sexes share incubation for 15 days, when the young hatch. In addition to the diet described for the preceding species, insects, fruits, berries, milk-softened white bread, and greens should be given.

The flock pigeon (*Phaps [Histriophaps] histrionica*) (also called flock-bronzewing or harlequin) from inland Australia, may occasionally still be seen in zoos and bird gardens. In Australia, where they once inhabited the whole continent in great numbers, they have become very scarce, with small flocks now occurring only in the north. The introduction of sheep and rabbits is thought to be largely responsible for their demise. The birds are readily recognizable by the head markings: a white forehead and chin on a dark blue-black head; the ear coverts are edged in white. There is a further white neck band. The breast is light gray; the rest of the body light brown, whitish-beige on the underside. The dark primary feathers are spotted with white.

Crested Pigeon (*Ocyphaps lophotes*) (2 subspecies)
(Other names: Crested Bronzewing, Topknot Pigeon)

Characteristics: Similar in size to the Barbary dove, the cock and hen are identical in appearance. The long pointed crest is black and the head gray. The breast and belly are gray. The red neck band is striking. The back is dark brown, with white spots and patches near the tail. The wings are light greenish-gray. The plumage of the head and breast has a pink sheen that shows off beautifully in the sun. The eyes are brownish-yellow, the orbital ring is red, the beak is black, and the feet are deep red. Length: 12 inches (30 cm); weight 4 ounces (115 g).

Natural Range and Behavior: Most of Australia except for the rain forest zones in the northern parts of the continent, the extreme southeast and Tasmania, and the extreme southwest. They prefer drier terrain, but never too far from water. During periods of drought thousands of these pigeons may be seen converging on still productive water sources. The fragile nest is built usually fairly low down in a thickly foliaged shrub. In some areas the bird widely uses the introduced pest shrub *Lantana* in which to nest. Though supposedly a protected species in Australia, the bird is regarded as good game, especially with regard to its rapid flight.

Care and Breeding: This beautiful pigeon is kept in both cages and aviaries, but in view of its love for fast flying it is better in a large aviary. In the wild, the flight path is direct and accompanied by whistling wing beats, caused by the specially narrowed third primary feather. Breeding poses no particular problems and the species is suitable for beginners as well as experienced fanciers. To avoid fighting, pairs should be kept separate from each other and from other dove species. Cocks are aggressive in and out of the breeding season, but they will usually live happily together with finches or similar unrelated birds. The flimsy nest is constructed on a platform or in a basket, from narrow twigs, straw, and the like. The hen lays two

eggs that are incubated for about 18 days, and the young are ready to leave the nest after two weeks. Sometimes the parents look after the young for four to five weeks after fledging. After three months the young are fully grown, and they are ready for breeding at 12 months.

It is recommended that a narrow perching plank be affixed around the upper walls of the aviary; bronzewing pigeons will also use such a plank, especially when it rains. Incidentally, crested pigeons make good foster parents for bronzewings.

The birds should be fed with various millet varieties, hemp, canary seed, poppy seed, wheat, and a variety of greens, plus grass seeds (very important, as this is more or less their staple diet in the wild). In the past there were several attempts to naturalize the crested pigeon in Europe, each time without success, even though the attempts were performed under the direction of leading ornithologists/aviculturists (Duke of Bedford, Dr. J. Delacour, Dr. J. Nicolai for example). Modern concepts of ecology and conservation now discourage the release of species into alien habitats.

Breeding crested pigeons poses no particular problems. A narrow perching plank should be affixed around the upper wall of the aviary.

Especially in Europe, but also in the United States, the crested pigeon is the most popular aviary dove after the diamond dove. It is a hardy species, and as long as it has access to a draft-proof and damp-proof night shelter, it can be kept in an outdoor aviary all year round. During the breeding season, but also frequently at other times, this species is intolerant towards its own and other dove species—whatever the size and planting of the aviary (like those for the *Phaps* species, see page 74). The crested pigeon has a habit of jumping onto the back of its rival (or any other dove) and pecking so violently that serious injuries, even fatalities will occur. It is thus also important to separate juveniles from their parents as soon as they are independent. Most fanciers keep their crested pigeons in single pairs, and never with other dove species, though finches and gallinaceous birds seem to be acceptable. Frequently, a pheasant or quail aviary is "decorated" with a pair of crested pigeons; the same may go for the aviary containing Australian grass finches.

In spite of the similar appearance of the sexes, it is usually quite easy to distinguish a cock from a hen by the aggressiveness of the cock, even out of the breeding season. A cock will assume an aggressive posture on seeing another crested pigeon (male or female; it doesn't matter), or another dove species. Although both sexes normally carry the crest upright, this is laid back on the neck during sleep, during courtship, during territorial aggression, or when the cock wants to attract a hen to a nesting site. In the latter case he also utters a cracking sound; a "gou, gou, gou"—like small twigs breaking. His body also makes rhythmic, rocking movements—a habit that we can also see in the young on the nest, or in the early fledgling period, as they beg for food; they even utter the "cracking" noises.

The courtship display of the cock is altogether captivating; he bows quickly several times to his chosen one, spreads his tail like a fan, and holds his wings away from the body. With this dance, he utters a short "woe" call.

White-bellied Plumed Pigeon (*Petrophassa [Lophophaps] plumifera*) (2 subspecies)

(Other names: Plumed Dove, Red Plumed Dove, Red Plumed Pigeon, Ground Dove)

Characteristics: Somewhat smaller than the Barbary dove, it has a characteristic killdeer-like chestnut brown crest; the general color of the body is also chestnut brown with black-banded blue feathers, giving the impression of a quail pattern. The belly is white and there is a black-edged white breast band. There is a bluish-gray eyebrow stripe, separated from the red orbital area by a black stripe. Below the eye there is a white patch that runs behind the eye and to the chin, where it is edged with black. The black marking merges into a blue-gray fleck. The beak is almost black, the iris yellowish, and the feet purplish-black. Length: 8 inches (21 cm); weight: 4 to 4⅛ ounces (115 to 117 g).

Natural Range and Behavior: Central and inland northern Australia, in stony and rocky habitats with spinifex growth. Always fairly close to water. Typical ground dwellers that live in loose flocks but in spite of this are aggressive toward each other. They run like partridges, though they are not excessively shy, even towards humans. They have a rapid, whirring flight.

Care and Breeding: They were first imported by the Amsterdam Zoo (Artis) in 1865. The birds need a large and especially dry aviary, without coinhabitants. The shelter and the covered part of the flights should have a thick layer of dry sand, decorated with a number of rocks and flat stones. This species always spends the night on the ground.

Courtship display is similar to that of the crested pigeon. An interesting observation was made by J. Anzenberger at a Belgian breeder's establishment. Several pairs of the birds were kept together in a large aviary. At a given moment, the cocks assembled in the middle of the floor and made a ring facing each other and bowing toward the center of the ring! The birds prepare nests in shallow scrapes made next to a rock or a grass clump. The hen lays two eggs. Breeding can be difficult as some birds have a nasty habit of pecking the eggs open or of abandoning them. Barbary doves are therefore often used as foster parents after ensuring that the laying times have been synchronized. The incubation time is 17 days. The young leave the nest as early as ten days later. The nest platform should be low as the young cannot fly when they leave the nest. Protect them from the cold at night with a warm cloth shield.

Partridge Bronzewing or Squatter Pigeon (*Petrophassa [Geophaps] scripta*) (2 subspecies).

Characteristics: Somewhat smaller than the feral pigeon, it has a striking black head marking. Mainly brown, it has a bluish-gray breast and belly that merges into white along the sides. There is a beautiful, metallic-green sheen on the wings. The beak is black, the orbital ring gray-blue, the iris dark brown, and the feet are reddish-purple. Length: 11 inches (28 cm); weight: 7¾ ounces (220 g).

Natural Range and Behavior: The northeastern and eastern parts of Australia. Because of the nature of their habitat, these birds spend much of their time on the ground. When alarmed they form a circle with their heads directed outwards. The nest is usually made on the ground and is little more than a shallow scrape, lined with a few leaves, stems, and roots.

The two eggs are incubated for 16 to 17 days and the young soon leave the nest but stay within the group. The young from each brood of a particular year stay together with the parents as a family group until the beginning of the next season. When the family sleep at night, they snuggle together, again with the heads directed outwards, in order to quickly detect danger; this is a habit that one can also see in quails, especially the Chinese painted quail (*Excalfactoria chinensis*).

Care and Breeding: First seen in the London Zoo in 1883, the squatter pigeon was bred a year later in France. These days, unfortunately, this species is rarely seen outside Australia. The same can be said for the closely related bare-eyed partridge bronzewing (*P. (G.) smithii*) from the Kimberley district of western Australia, and the Northern Territory; this species was first imported into Germany in 1903 and was bred (by Lecailles) again in France, in 1922. The slightly smaller white-quilled rock pigeon (*P. albipennis*), from the Kimberley district of western Australia, is also rarely seen in captivity in Europe and the United States though there are some enthusiastic breeders in its native land.

The shy bare-eyed partridge bronzewing (Petrophassa [Geophaps] smithii) "freezes," remaining inconspicuous when disturbed on the ground. The species flies in short, swift bursts close to the ground.

The wonga pigeon (Leucosarcia melanoleuca) lives mainly on the ground but constructs its nest high in a tree.

gray with a light yellow forehead and a white neck band, and the underside has sparse checkered markings. The beak is reddish with a black tip, the narrow orbital ring is red, the iris dark brown, and the feet red. Length: 12 inches (30 cm); weight: about 17⅝ ounces (500 g).

Natural Range and Behavior: An inhabitant of the rain forests of eastern Australia. The bird lives mainly on the ground, but makes its nest high in a tree. The food consists of seeds, fruits, berries, and insects.

Care and Breeding: This splendid pigeon was first seen in the Antwerp Zoo (Belgium) in 1845, and in 1859 in the London Zoo. It was bred in London in the same year. In the 1860s and 1870s it was introduced by Dutch and Belgian importers to many parts of Europe and North America; it is especially popular as a zoo exhibit. This species is quite tolerant, has no particular breeding difficulties and can stay outside for the winter providing it has access to a draft-proof and damp-proof shelter. Some fanciers complain

Wonga Pigeon (*Leucosarcia melanoleuca*)

Characteristics: This well-known, much kept dove is about the same size and weight as a wood pigeon. It has strikingly short wings and tail. The bird stands high on its legs. It is mainly

The wonga pigeon is quite tolerant and can stay outside for the winter, providing it has access to an adequate shelter.

about this pigeon's monotonous call. A choice of baskets or platforms in a thick shrub should be offered for nesting. The diet is as described for the bronzewings (see page 74).

Genus: *Geopelia*

The popular, almost domesticated diamond dove belongs to this well-known genus. Members of the genus can be said to resemble the turtledove, *Streptopelia turtur,* but it is more likely that they have resulted as a split from the tree doves of the genus *Henicophaps* (bronze-winged doves). This relationship can be seen more closely in their courtship behavior—for example, the raising and spreading of the tail and the bowing of the head.

Diamond Dove, *Geopelia* (sometimes *Strictopelia*) *cuneata* (2 subspecies)

Characteristics: One of the smallest doves (not much bigger than a mouse) that is aviculturally very popular. The common name bespeaks the narrowly black-bordered white spots on the wings (wing coverts as well as secondaries) and shoulders, which are otherwise gray-blue. These white "diamonds" are very conspicuous and contribute to the charming appearance of these peaceful little doves. The cock has a darker head, neck, and breast than the hen, in which the throat and mantle have a brownish tone. The cock's back is light brown. The four middle tail feathers are dark gray with black tips; the other tail feathers have white tips. The lower belly and undertail feathers are white. The orbital ring is coral red, the iris orange-red, the beak olive-brown and the feet flesh-colored.

Sexes can be difficult to distinguish, but the cock has a somewhat larger head and wider orbital rings. One positive sign is the courtship dance of the cock. Length: 7½ inches (19 cm); weight: 1½ ounces (45 g).

Natural Range and Behavior: The diamond dove occurs mainly in central and northern Australia where it inhabits open terrain (mulga scrub), but it sometimes lives in towns and cities where it may be seen in parks and gardens but never far from water. They are fast fliers and frequently let out their soft "coo-coo" call.

It is interesting to watch the courtship dance of the male. With a fanned-out tail he circles around the hen and repeatedly lets out his loud, sometimes irritating call. Both birds share in the incubation of the two eggs which hatch in 13 to 14 days. As soon as they are independent, the young should be removed from the aviary, for sooner or later they will be attacked by the parents, who may wish to start another brood.

Care and Breeding: Diamond doves are kept extensively in both indoor and outdoor aviaries, and it is possible to keep a pair successfully in a large cage. For most of the day they will forage on the ground or sit on a

The diamond dove (Geopelia cuneata) is one of the most popular cage and aviary birds. It is easily managed and very suitable in a mixed collection of seed-eating species.

The whitetail diamond dove is one of the latest mutations.

nest box sunning themselves. Pairs will breed very readily and one or two eggs are laid. As good pairs can be difficult to obtain, inbreeding is often utilized. This is not too dangerous as long as it is not done too often. One way of avoiding excessive imbreeding is by arrangement with fellow fanciers whereby birds can be "borrowed" and offspring can be shared.

The birds are quite hardy and can often stay outside all winter as long as they have a damp-proof and draft-proof shelter. In very cold weather, however, they are best kept locked in the shelter as they tend to sit for long periods in one spot. Outdoors in winter they could get frostbite or colds. As an extra precaution it is perhaps best to keep them in an unheated indoor area (such as in the garage or in the loft) during the winter.

The nest platform can consist of mesh or wood; even half a coconut shell may suffice! A few twigs and leaf veins will serve as nest material; they are mad about tobacco leaf veins—a material that will even keep lice away!

In addition, a little moss and grass will be used to construct a basic nest.

Often a pair of diamond doves refuse to breed. I believe that most such pairs consist of birds that have been intensively inbred. Therefore it is worth repeating: inbreeding is acceptable, but don't overdo it! Experience has shown that a single pair in an aviary will often produce better results than several pairs together. A maximum of four broods per year should be allowed.

As these birds are so easy to keep, they are ideal for beginners. Diamond doves can be given a mixture of sorghum, millet, canary seed, weed and grass seeds, poppy and rape seeds, and the like. Also offer regular universal food, water-soaked or milk-soaked stale bread, ant pupae, small mealworms, enchytrae (whiteworms), a rich assortment of greens, cuttlefish bone, and grit. Fresh, clean water, of course, should never be missing.

Try to have the birds spend the night in the shelter, as they are quickly scared and may panic the other birds in the aviary, sometimes with unpleasant consequences.

Recently a number of color mutations have been bred, of which the "silver" (light silver-gray) is probably the most popular. There is also a wholly white variety, and a dark gray with a lot of brown in the plumage ("brown"). From South Africa we got the "yellow," the "cinnamon," and the "pied"; even a "red" is available.

Bar-shouldered Dove (*Geopelia humeralis*) (3 subspecies)

(Other names: Mangrove Dove, Pandanus Pigeon)

Characteristics: Similar in size to the Barbary dove, the cock is largely sky-blue-gray; the neck is beige with black edges to the feathers. The underbody is light red, the belly is white. The narrow wings (the birds are excellent fliers), like the tail, are brown. The hen is grayer on the breast and generally more somberly colored. The eyes are yellowish to green, the orbital ring is blue-gray, the beak is grayish-blue, and the feet are rose-red. Length: about 10 inches (26 cm); weight: 4 ounces (115 g).

Natural Range and Behavior: Northern and eastern Australia; a darker-colored subspecies exists in New Guinea, and a lighter one in western Australia. These doves like to stay close to water, especially coastal mangrove forests, but may turn up in any areas where there is fresh water.

Care and Breeding: These rather expensive but attractive doves spend most of their time on the ground, running from one corner to the next, following each other closely, flying a few meters away, pecking up some suitable seed; always on the move! They are not particularly restless or nervous, however, but spry and vivacious, suited to a large community aviary. They are very hardy and quickly become tame, soon learning to take treats from your hand. Once accustomed to a seasonal climate, they can be kept in an outdoor aviary all year round, providing it has a well-protected shelter. The diet is similar to that described for the peaceful dove (see page 85); the only difference is that these birds like to eat occasional insects.

You will understand that such lively birds as these are not suited to cages or small aviaries, but they will feel at home where they have adequate freedom of movement. They will also breed more readily in a larger aviary if provided with a choice of small boxes or half coconut shells. The one or two young hatch after 22 days of incubation. These grow very quickly and leave the nest in 10 to 12 days. You should keep the breeding pairs separate from their own or other dove species, since the males can be quite aggressive.

The bar-shouldered dove (Geopelia humeralis) is a very hardy, lively and spry bird. It becomes tame quickly.

The female of the zebra or barred ground dove (Geopelia striata) is usually slightly smaller. It is a very prolific species.

Zebra Dove (*Geopelia striata*) (6 subspecies)

Characteristics: Similar in size to the diamond dove, the forehead and throat of the cock are soft-gray. The neck is rose-red, as is the breast. There are some narrow black and white stripes on the breast and throat, neck, and cheeks. The lower underbody is white, the wings are brown with black bands. The tail is black with white spots. The eyes and the beak are grayish-brown, the feet light red. The hen is difficult to distinguish, but sometimes is smaller (this, of course, applies only if you have comparative specimens). The hen is perhaps a little more somberly patterned and colored. Length: about 8½ inches (22 cm); weight: 1¾ ounces (50 g).

Natural Range and Behavior: Southeast Asia and the Indonesian Archipelago. They spend a great deal of the day on the ground, browsing for seeds and insects. They live in the more open habitats, with stands of trees and shrubs. The courtship display is similar to that of the diamond dove.

Care and Breeding: First imported by the Berlin Zoo in 1845, this charming and colorful dove has increased in popularity in recent years. Its relatively easy breeding make it well worth keeping. The breeding methods are similar to those described for the diamond dove; it is only sometimes difficult to make up a true pair, in view of the difficulty in distinguishing the sexes. When buying these birds it is thus always best to get an agreement with the seller to change a bird if necessary. You can be sure you have a true pair only when you first see the cock's courtship display.

According to some fanciers, the zebra dove is not very interesting in the community aviary, but I have found that a pair can give you much pleasure. Indeed, they are not particularly lively, but they move peacefully about and stealthily view the activity around them. Occasionally, but not very often, they may sit in a particular spot for hours. As long as you have lively coinhabitants in the aviary, the doves are likely to interact, with minor squabbles and acrobatics. I find them quiet even in the breeding period, but you must ensure that they are not alarmed; they are very sensitive to sudden disturbances. For success in the breeding season, therefore, peace and quiet must be the order of the day. Experience has shown that these birds must be kept in a warm station indoors during the winter.

Peaceful Dove (*Geopelia [placida] striata tranquilla*) (*G. placida*) (2 subspecies)

(Other names: Zebra Dove, Turtledove)

Characteristics: Similar in size to the diamond dove, the cock is beautifully colored, with mainly gray cheeks, throat, and crown. The back of the head is brownish. There is a wavy, dark brown pattern on the back. The breast shows a striking, blood-red sheen. The lower underside is grayish-white. The narrow neck has wavy white and brown stripes. The hen is very similar to the cock, but perhaps a little slighter in build. Length: 8 inches (20 cm); weight: 1¾ ounces (50 g).

Natural Range and Behavior: Northern and eastern Australia, and central western Australia. The birds mainly inhabit sparsely treed grasslands, where they forage for seeds on the ground. I have seen these birds also in large gardens and parks. They build their nests high up in a tree—18 feet (6 m) or more.

Care and Breeding: Experience has shown that these birds will thrive and breed in a modest room aviary, as well as a large outdoor one, but the best breeding results occur in the latter. In comparison to other doves and even other exotic birds, these are about the least difficult. I even had a pair, of which the cock regularly took food from my fingers. Peaceful doves should not be kept in community with other ground-dwelling birds, as they are intolerant of continual harassment from such birds as quails or partridges; in my experience, these doves are more subject to bullying than other dove species. It is also advisable not to keep other larger or aggressive birds together with them.

The diet consists of various millet varieties, canary seed, a little crushed hemp, and, prior to and during the breeding season, all kinds of seeding grasses and herbaceous plants. When young are in the nest, it is a good idea to offer soaked seed. Rearing food, and old white bread softened in milk is also eagerly accepted. Peaceful doves are perhaps not such problem-free breeders as diamond doves, but they will usually nest in a half coconut shell or a little box 5 × 10 × 2 inches (12 × 25 × 6 cm). It is best to give them a start for the nest by putting some thin twigs, straw, and roots in the platform; they will then construct a simple nest from these. Warning! Disturb the birds as little as possible, and they will raise one or two young per brood.

During the winter months these birds should be taken to a warm spot indoors. I have bred this species several times; they used the nesting facilities provided in the night shelter. I placed heat lamps close to the nest and left them permanently switched on; these beautiful birds are great lovers of warmth. In the wild they build their nests, as I have seen, so that the incubating bird can be in sunshine for as long as possible. That is why we give them the extra warmth in captivity. Further care is as described for the diamond dove (see page 81).

Genera *Zenaida, Nesopelia,* and *Melopelia*

These genera can all be placed under the general English name of mourning doves. As a group, these birds are relatively small, mainly brown, and all fairly similar in appearance; for this reason, I have grouped them together here. All of the species have small glossy patches on the neck, a black cheek stripe, and black wing patches. Members of the genera have a good reputation in aviculture, being not difficult to breed.

Mourning Dove (*Zenaida macroura*) (6 subspecies)

(Other name: Carolina Dove)

Characteristics: A little smaller than the Barbary dove; also more

The mourning dove (Zenaida macroura) is a very common species, occurring from southern Canada to western Panama and on some islands of the Caribbean.

slender and with a longer tail. The cock has a brown head and a gray crown. The neck is also gray. There is a black patch beneath the eye. The throat is brownish-yellow. The breast is a strikingly reddish color, with a few purple patches. The lower underparts are off-white, the back brown. The wings are also brown, but have black stripes. The eyes are brown, the orbital ring is slate-gray, the beak is black with red, the feet are deep red. The hen is somewhat slighter in build and is grayer in color beneath. Length: about 12 inches (30 cm); weight: 5 ounces (140 g).

Natural Range and Behavior: North and Central America, Cuba, the Bahamas, Isle of Pines, and Hispaniola. It lives mainly in lightly wooded areas, also in parks and gardens. Landowners are not fond of this species as it has been blamed for some agricultural damage. This species seems to be closely related to the extinct American passenger pigeon. In the United States the Carolina dove is presently the most abundant wild dove.

Care and Breeding: They are hardy and quite easy to breed doves, with simple requirements. This, however, is not to say that we should be less vigilant in their care; with thoughtful breeding we can produce splendid youngsters, for which there will be a ready market.

The "shaky" nest is built about 3 feet (1 m) high in a thickly foliaged shrub with strong twigs. I like to place a platform of wood or mesh under the nest to avoid loss of eggs or young. The hen lays two eggs and the incubation time is about 13 days. The young fledge after 16 to 17 days. They must be kept indoors during the winter. Z. m. macroura, from Cuba, is occasionally available. Diet: millet, canary seed, and so on.

My tip: In the wild, mouring doves generally feed on the ground. To put my specimens at ease, I always provide large, open floor patches.

Galapagos Dove (Nesopelia galapagoensis) (2 subspecies)

Characteristics: Somewhat smaller and plumper than the Barbary dove. The general impression of this brilliant dove, which stands high on its legs, is chocolate-brown with a wine-red sheen. The underside is paler in color. The wings have black and white stripes. The primaries are black, with narrow white edges. The head and neck are wine-red. The beak is black, the orbital ring is blue, the iris is brown, and the feet are purple-red. Length: 5 inches (13 cm); weight: 2⅝ to 3½ ounces (80 to 100 g).

The mourning dove seems to be closely related to the extinct American passenger pigeon.

Galapagos doves are best kept as single pairs in their own aviary.

Natural Range and Behavior: The coastal areas of the Galapagos Islands. These birds are typical ground dwellers, as can be seen by their strong legs and broad feet. They poke around in the volcanic earth in search of food. The flight is quite rapid and they often fly from one island to another. The flimsy nests are constructed in crevices and hollows among the rocks. Two eggs are laid; they are incubated for 17 days.

Care and Breeding: This bird was first shown in the London Zoo in 1893; it was first bred around 1922 by A. E. Colburn in Los Angeles. In Europe, the legendary Jean Delacour first bred this species in 1934. With thoughtful care, a pair of these birds will bring good breeding results. Unfortunately there is a mistaken belief that this species is winter-hardy, and as this is far from fact, many birds have been lost. During late fall and winter the birds must be brought into a slightly warmed indoor aviary. The floor of the aviary should have a thick layer of dry sand, decorated with a few flat rocks, which will be used as resting perches. The birds are best kept as single pairs in their own aviary, since they tend to be aggressive towards their own and other dove species. These doves have the habit of poking around in the ground for food, so it can happen that the seed dish is emptied in no time at all and the seed scattered over the aviary floor. Nicolai suggested that these birds should be given a long, shallow trough, with only a thin layer of seed in it. During courtship, the cock utters a very soft call, while he follows his bride with his feathers fluffed; occasionally he stands motionless with his beak pointed almost vertically downward. Next, he lures the hen toward the nest site by bowing the front part of his body deeply, moving his spread tail feathers from side to side, and fluttering his wings. Before copulation, the pair peck each other behind the wings (Nicolai). Then the cock feeds the hen with increasing regurgitative actions and finally flies onto her back so that pairing can be completed.

Although the young fledge when they are ready to fly, they usually spend several days on the ground, returning to the nest at night. The diet consists of a variety of millets, canary seed, and good commercial canary seed mixture, rearing food and egg food for canaries and a rich variety of greens. Hens are sexually mature at three and a half months; cocks at four

The Galapagos dove (Nesopelia galapagoensis) likes to poke around in the volcanic earth in search of food.

months. For maximum success, the birds should be kept where the temperature does not fall below 68°F (20°C). Many experienced fanciers keep these birds in an indoor aviary, although there is no reason that they cannot be kept in an outdoor aviary during late spring and summer, as long as they have a well-insulated, dry night shelter. A deep sandy substrate decorated with flat rocks is strongly recommended.

White-winged Dove (*Melopelia [Zenaidura] asiatica*)

Characteristics: Somewhat larger than the Barbary dove. The crown, neck, and nape are dull pink; the forehead, throat, and breast gold-brown; grayer in the area of the beak. The lower throat is white. There is a black patch behind the ear, followed by a bronze patch. The wings are rust-brown, the back and upper tail coverts are gray-blue. The central tail feathers are reddish-brown, while the outers are blue-gray with black edges. There is a white wing band that is visible only when the bird is resting, thus with closed wings. The underside is gray-blue. The beak is black, the broad orbital ring bluish, the iris orange-red, and the feet red. Length: 4½ inches (11.5 cm); weight: 3⅞ ounces (109 g).

Natural Range and Behavior: Southern United States and the whole of Central America to Panama and Costa Rica. Also in the southern Bahamas (Great Inagua Island), Cuba, Jamaica, and Hispaniola. This dove is also common in South America, in southwestern Ecuador, Peru, and northern Chile. The birds inhabit mainly dry, lightly wooded areas, but also agricultural land, large gardens, and parks. In Panama, I saw it in the mangroves. The birds spend a great deal of time on the ground.

Care and Breeding: This species was first imported to England in 1901. The two eggs are incubated for 18 days; the young fledge after three to four weeks. They are especially fond of berries. For further details on care and breeding see the Galapagos dove.

Genera *Columbina, Metriopelia, and Scardafella*

These small American ground doves occur in the southern United States, Central America, and in a large part of South America. The body is compact and the tail is short. They are mainly brown and gray, and mostly have a black or metallic patch on the wings.

Scaly-breasted Ground Dove (*Columbina passerina*) (18 subspecies)

Characteristics: Similar in size to the diamond dove. The cock has a wine-red forehead, sides of head, and breast, with a scaly pattern on the head, breast, and sides of the neck. The belly is reddish, merging into whitish near the tail. The back is gray-brown, and the wings have black markings. The primaries are reddish-brown with black tips. The central tail feathers are gray-brown with white edges. The beak is red, pink, or flesh-colored, with a black tip, the iris is orange to dark brown, and the feet are light red. Length: 7½ inches (19 cm); weight: 1½ ounces (45 g).

Natural Range and Behavior: Southern United States, Central America, West Indian Islands to Ecuador, and northern Brazil. These doves are largely ground dwelling in the low coastal shrubberies, in light woodland or in mangrove forest, sometimes in gardens or parks. After initial shyness they quickly become tame and in some areas (parks, parking lots, etc.) will take seeds or bread from almost beneath your feet.

Care and Breeding: As for the diamond dove.

White-winged doves are very fond of berries.

Plain-breasted Ground Dove (*Columbina minute*) (3 subspecies)

Characteristics: Similar in size to the diamond dove, the cock is mainly gray and gray-brown. There is a vague reddish sheen on the forehead. The throat and breast are red. The lower underbody is off-white. The beak is brown, the eyes are red, and the feet are rose-red. The hen is light gray and brown above, the throat and belly are white, the breast and flanks brownish-gray; the hen thus has no red in her plumage, except a vague shimmer on the forehead. Length: about 7½ inches (19 cm); weight: 1⅞ ounces (45 g).

Natural Range and Behavior: Peru and Brazil, where they prefer to forage on the ground, only ascending into the

The Inca dove breeds readily in a roomy aviary.

Scaly doves love sun-basking and a thick layer of sand on the aviary floor.

trees to roost. The relatively large nest is round; it is built from grass and twigs, usually on the bare ground. There is a hollow in the middle to contain the eggs. The birds are found on grass-lands, forest edges, and farmland.

Care and Breeding: This is a commonly kept species that requires similar husbandry to that of the diamond dove (see page 81). As these are relatively peaceful doves and because they have pleasant calls, these doves rapidly win the hearts of fanciers and are often kept in indoor aviaries. They quickly become tame, although at first they are very nervous, hanging on the aviary wire and flying into it. After a few days they settle well and will soon be accepting treats from your fingers. They breed fairly easily; many fanciers place their eggs under diamond doves, that are well known for their fostering prowess. This method does have its good points, but you

have to take into consideration the fact that the foster parents must be at the same stage of breeding as the biological parents. As we know, doves feed their young with so-called crop milk. The makeup of the crop milk is closely connected with the age of the young and, after a few days, it is largely replaced by partially digested feed that is ideal for the older nestlings. If we place hatchling doves with foster parents who are at this later stage, the hatchlings will be inadequately fed and will probably not survive. The incubation time is 16 days. The cock and the hen share in incubation, the hen usually in the night and mornings, the cock during the day. It is best to separate the young from the parents as soon as they are independent (usually at about one month of age). Four broods a year are not unusual; more are not recommended.

The **picui dove** (*Columbina picui*), which is also tolerant of other doves and comes from southeastern Brazil, Argentina, Uruguay, and central Chile, requires the same kind of husbandry as the white-winged dove. The **bare-faced ground dove** (*Metriopelia ceciliae*), from Peru, Bolivia, and Northern Chile, is an interesting species that is occasionally imported and also requires similar care. Place thick branches and platforms against the aviary walls, and the doves will rest on these for hours. They are extremely active ground-loving birds.

Inca Dove (*Scardafella inca*)

Characteristics: Somewhat larger than the diamond dove, this species is largely grayish-brown; light gray on the forehead, white on the throat. The neck and head are light pinkish-brown, the breast if dull pink, and the rest of the underbody yellowish-white. All the feathers have dark gray edges, except those of the head and breast. The beak is black, the iris orange-red, and the feet pink. Length: 7½ inches (19 cm); weight: 1 ounce (30 g).

Natural Range and Behavior: Arizona, New Mexico, and Texas, Central America (to Nicaragua), and northwestern Costa Rica. This species is generally present in most types of terrain, but preferably open fields, parks, and gardens; they like to be near human habitations. The two eggs are incubated for 14 days and the young leave the nest at 14 to 16 days of age.

Care and Breeding: These birds will breed readily in an aviary. Small baskets or canary nesting pans may be used as a nest foundation. At first, Inca doves are shy, but they can become very tame after a few months; in any case, they are more trusting than the **scaly dove,** (*S. squamata*), from Colombia, Venezuela, the Margarita Islands, and Trinidad. Both species require similar care. They love sun basking and it will help if they have a thick layer of sand on the aviary floor. During the winter they must be kept in a warm spot indoors. Newly imported birds are shy and nervous, often hide in the shrubs, and spend the night in a nest box. The scaly dove was first imported by the London Zoo in 1867 and was first bred by Seth-Smith (England) in 1904.

Genus *Leptotila*

These tall standing doves come from Central and South America. They have a relatively short tail that consists of ten feathers. They spend a lot of time on the ground, where they forage for food. When danger threatens, they disappear into thick foliage.

Caribbean or White-bellied Dove (*Leptotila jamaicensis*) (4 subspecies)

Characteristics: This species is a little larger than the Barbary dove. The forehead and underside are white. The crown is gray, and the back of the head has a bronze sheen. There is a violet-blue sheen on the neck. The wings are greenish-brown. The gray-brown tail feather have white tips, except for the two central ones. The beak is black, the orbital ring purple, the iris is gray with a red border, and the feet are red. Length: 5½ inches (14 cm); weight: 4⅛ to 4¼ ounces (117 to 120 g).

Natural Range and Behavior: Jamaica, northern Yucatan, Grand Cayman Island, St. Andrew, Coizumel, Holbox Island, and Megeres Island. They prefer open areas with scattered stands of trees. They live mainly on the ground and can run at great speed, with the head held back, especially if danger threatens; the tail is first held down and later held up. The hen lays three eggs and the incubation time is 15 days. The nest is placed low down in thick foliage.

Care and Breeding: This species was first imported by the Berlin Zoo in 1845. It does not require much in the way of cereals, but should be offered hemp, finely chopped peanuts, various millets, mealworms, and similar high protein foods, canary egg food, a rich variety of berries, and pieces of fruit (apple, pear, etc.). The bird requires warmth during the winter.

Genera *Geotrygon* and *Staroenas*

Members of these genera are native to Central and South America. they are "long-legged" inhabitants of the woodlands that spend most of their time on the ground, but roost in a tree at night. Unfortunately they are seldom imported at present, although the better zoos usually have a few pairs on display.

Gray-faced Quail Dove (*Geotrygon caniceps*) (2 subspecies)

Characteristics: Similar in size to the Barbary dove, it has a whitish-gray head, almost pure white on the forehead. The sides of the breast and the whole back are bluish-violet with a black sheen, merging into dark blue near the tail. The breast and underside are dark gray; the lower belly undertail coverts are reddish-brown. The beak is dark red with a horn-colored tip, the iris is orange-red, and the feet are dull red. Length: 4¾ inches (12 cm); weight: about 4 ounces (112 to 115 g).

Natural Range and Behavior: Cuba; the somewhat darker and more metallic-looking subspecies *G. c. leucometopsis* occurs on the island of Hispaniola. Members of the Cuban strain live in the lowland tropical forests, while the Hispaniolan strain occurs in the rain forests. With deforestation and associated degradation of the land, the Cuban strain is seriously threatened and extinction is not out of the question unless something is done soon! The hen lays only one dark cream-colored egg.

Care and Breeding: First imported into France in 1923 and in the same year successfully bred by Madame Lecallier. The young hatches after 13 days, and leaves the nest after 12 days. At the present time this species is most uncommon in captivity. They require adequate warmth, and must be given warmed accommodation in winter.

It is really time that zoological and avicultural parks and serious fanciers cooperate to develop a breeding program for this captivating and beautiful dove, before it is too late! The birds will require a large aviary, with a layer of pine needles and river sand on the floor, and planted with a few thickly foliaged shrubs. These doves are extremely lively and are fond of animal-based food (mealworms, white-worms, earthworms, nonhairy caterpillars, slugs, ant pupae, and so on); also canary egg food, hemp, crushed sunflower seeds, finely chopped peanuts, pine nuts (very important), milo, niger, canary seed, finely chopped fruit (especially apple and pear), and a rich variety of greens. Small baskets as nest foundations should be placed about 3 to 6 feet (1 to 2 m) high in the thick shrubs.

The **crested quail dove,** or **mountain witch** (so named by the local natives because the call of the cock in the mating season is said to resemble "the sighing of a dying man"), is also worth mention. The dove (*G. versicolor*) has a gray-black forehead, yellow cheeks, a chocolate-brown body, chestnut brown wings, a soft blue-gray breast, and a rust brown lower underside. The rump and tail are green-black. The head and especially the neck have a bronze sheen. The head feathers form a thick, short crest. The bird inhabits the thick lowland and

The name "mountain witch" comes from the call of the male in the mating season, which is said to resemble "the sighing of a dying man."

The bridled quail dove inhabits woodland and forest in dry localities with dense under-growth. The species feed on the ground, preferring snails and seeds.

The crested quail dove (Geotrygon versicolor) of Jamaica was first imported by the London Zoo in 1860. The species is known for its remarkable call.

montane forests of Jamaica. It was first imported by the London Zoo in 1860, and was first bred in 1901. The hen lays the usual two eggs, which are incubated for 13 days. Further care is the same as for the preceding species. The same goes for the Key West quail dove (*G. chrysia*) from Cuba, the Bahamas, and Hispaniola; the bridled quail dove (*G. mystacea*) from the Virgin Islands and the Lesser Antilles, and the ruddy quail dove (*G. montana*) from southern Mexico to western Paraguay and Misiones, Argentina, and the Greater and Lesser Antilles (in moist lowland forests, coffee, and cocoa plantations; but I have also seen them as high as 3,900 feet [1,300 m] in the mountains). In the aviary they have the habit of sitting on the edge of the water dish, head outwards, so that their droppings naturally fall in the water. The water must therefore be changed as frequently as possible. The species (*G. montana*) is one of the most friendly and trusting doves I know; when you enter the aviary, they will gather around your feet or land on your shoulder, arm, or head, in search of affection.

Blue-headed Quail Dove, or Cuba Bluehead (*Staroenas cyanocephala*)

Characteristics: Similar in size to the Barbary dove, with shorter legs than the other quail doves. The crown is slate-gray, marked with a black band that runs "through the eye" and edges the upper side of the eyebrow. Under this band is a white stripe. The back and tail are dark greenish-brown. The wings are dark brown. The throat and upper part of the breast are black, marked with a white breast band. The breast is wine-red. The beak is red with a dark gray tip; the iris is a dark brown, the feed are red. Length: 5 inches (13 cm); weight: about 4 ounces (112 to 115 g).

Natural Range and Behavior: Cuba. Those released at the beginning of the century in Jamaica all died out, unfortunately, a long time ago.

The ruddy quail dove (Geotrygon montana) can be seen as high as 4,000 feet in the mountains.

The bird inhabits mainly lowland forest, but I have seen them high on rocky mountains. Mainly ground dwellers, they prefer to nest in low trees or shrubs, sometimes on the ground. The hen lays two eggs. I have no further details with regard to the breeding of this species.

Care and Breeding: It was already imported into England in 1794 and in 1854 in the Netherlands (Artis). The first breeding success was reported by the London Zoo in 1870. With continual deforestation and human predation, this species is declining seriously in numbers, and may even be threatened with extinction. Because of its short legs, it moves slowly. It must have slightly warmed winter accommodations. It is tolerant and peaceful towards other doves. The Barbary dove is often used as a foster parent for this species. In 1965, breeder Schneider (California) bred 12 youngsters from two pairs!

The much-sought-after Nicobar pigeon (Caloenas nicobarica) is very rare in its range. It has long, sickle-shaped neck hackles, which form a sort of mane, and a small knob at the base of the bill. There are probably one or two colonies left in the wild.

Genus *Caloenas*

This genus has only one species. The dove is characterized by its long neck feathers, short tail, long, strong wings, long legs, and robust beak, which has a large fleshy, warty cere at its base.

Nicobar Pigeon (*Caloenas nicobarica*) (2 subspecies)

Characteristics: Similar in size to the wood pigeon, the general color of this species is dark metallic blue, with a greenish-blue sheen on the wings. Striking sickle-shaped neck hackles, which form a short will require a mane; white tail. Gray beak (see genus description), brown, sometimes white iris, and purple-red feet. The cere is smaller in the hen and she is also somewhat slighter in build. Length: 16⅛ inches (41 cm); weight: 21⅕ ounces (600 g).

Natural Range and Behavior: Nicobar Islands, Palau Islands, Greater and Lesser Sunda Islands, Philippines, Moluccas, New Guinea, Bismarck Islands, and Solomon Islands. Members of this species forage on the ground for food, and they nest in colonies. Sometimes they migrate long distances from island to island in search of a good food source. They feed largely on seeds, fruit, snails, and other invertebrates. They roost in trees at night. They are very active at dusk and dawn, both in the wild and in captivity. During the day, the birds sometimes take up a "vulture posture" on a high branch, surveying the surrounding area.

Care and Breeding: These birds were first imported into the Netherlands in the seventeenth century. They require a long aviary—minimum 18 feet (6 m). It is tolerant of other dove species as well as other birds in a colony aviary, even during the breeding season. The hen lays a single egg in a strong nest built among

The Nicobar pigeon, being a typical ground feeder, eats large seeds, fruits, and invertebrates. In captivity the species becomes active at dusk, but it feeds throughout the day in the wild.

Bartlett's bleeding-heart pigeons are much in demand. Like the bleeding-heart pigeon, this beautiful bird enjoys both rain and dust-bathing.

The numbers of the bleeding-heart pigeon (Gallicolumba luzonica) are decreasing. The female is somewhat smaller than the male.

the twigs and branches of a tree. Incubation time is 30 days, and the young stay in the nest for 3 months! The birds must have a roomy, slightly warmed, weatherproof shelter in the winter. The floor can be covered with a thick layer of sand; a number of thick branches should be supplied for perching. The diet consists of corn, hemp, peanuts, pine nuts, wheat, etc. A regular supply of dove grit is essential. Personally, I give them grit twice a week between 9 and 11 A.M.

Genus *Gallicolumba*

These ground doves, so well known to all fanciers of pigeons and doves, have a compact, quail-like body, with sturdy, rather long legs, short wings, and a fairly short tail. They need a fair amount of animal-based food.

Bleeding-heart Pigeon (*Gallicolumba luzonica*)

Characteristics: Similar in size to the wood pigeon, it has a striking breast patch resembling a bleeding wound. The upper parts are greenish-gray, with darker parts that, behind the head and the rump, merge into brown-gray. The underside is yellowish-white with a darker tone in the wings, which are really largely green-gray, with brown flight feathers that, with their black tips, suggest banding; the tail feathers are similar. The eyes and the beak are red to black-brown, the feet are purple-red. the red breast-patch in the hen is smaller and weaker in color than that of the cock. Length: about 10 inches (25 cm); weight: 5¼ to 7 ounces (150 to 200 g).

Natural Range and Behavior: Luzon and Polillo (Philippines), especially in thickly forested areas. Stays mainly on the ground, but will roost in a tree. The simple nest is built in a shrub or creeper. The two eggs are incubated for 17 days. The young leave the nest after 12 days and are already capable of flying.

Care and Breeding: This species is increasing in popularity. It is the red breast marking that always attracts and, of course, gives it its name. The birds are presently protected and can be kept only under license, unless they were already in your possession before the legislation.

Bleeding-heart doves were first imported in 1869 (London) but were in Berlin by the following year. In France, the doves were soon breeding, though the eggs were normally hatched and the young reared by foster parents. One breeder raised 20 young, from 24 eggs, in a single season. If you use the foster method, you must separate the sexes from October to April to prevent exhaustion in the hen.

The birds must be offered fly pupae, and hard food (seed, etc.) for doves. Some tame individuals will take small mealworms. Conditioning is not so easy, since these doves have a very nervous nature. At nights they can sometimes panic and fly against the aviary mesh, occasionally with unpleasant results. Peace and quiet is thus very important if you want success with these beautiful birds.

The courtship display is very interesting. The cock runs quickly after the hen with his tail dragging on the ground; then he suddenly stops, presses his tail hard against the ground, puffs his breast out (somewhat reminiscent of a pouter or cropper pigeon), and lets out a short "coohoo" call. The dance is accompanied by wing clapping, similar to the behavior of a begging juvenile. The nest is constructed preferably 32 to 100 inches (82 to 256 cm) above the ground in thick foliage. Ensure that you supply a choice of nesting sites. The cock carries the nesting materials (twigs, etc.), while the hen "arranges" them in a structure that barely deserves the name "nest." The two grayish-white eggs are incubated for about two weeks and the gray-colored young fledge just 12 days later.

In the wild, the nest is constructed quite often on the ground; not surprising for ground doves! In addition to a good seed mixture, the birds must have a regular supply of insect food, especially when the parents are no longer feeding the young with crop milk. Berries and oily seeds are also taken. For good success with these birds, it is important to give them the following seeds: hemp, crushed sunflower seeds, finely chopped peanuts, pine nuts, millet varieties, and crushed corn. Additionally we can give egg food, milk-soaked stale white bread, yogurt (mixed with rearing or universal food), mealworms, earthworms, snails, nonhairy caterpillars, all kinds of berries, chopped fruits, and a great variety of greens.

Bartlett's Bleeding-heart Pigeon (*Gallicolumba criniger*) (3 subspecies)

Characteristics: Somewhat larger than the preceding species, this bird has a dark gray forehead, and a metallic-green crown, neck, nape, and upper part of the back; the rest of the back is reddish-brown with a purplish tinge. The breast is white with an intensive red "bleeding-heart" patch. The underside is yellowish-white. Length: 11 inches (28 cm); weight: 7 ounces (200 g).

Natural Range and Behavior: Basilan, Leyte, Mindanao, and Samar (Philippines). Strictly confined to the forests.

Care and Breeding: This desirable dove is seldom seen in aviaries, except perhaps occasionally in the better zoos or bird parks. Interestingly, the cock does not spread the wings in the courtship display like the preceding species. The hen lays only one egg, which is incubated for 13 to 17

The Bartlett's bleeding-heart pigeon (Gallicolumba criniger) is very popular. Their clutch consists of only a single egg.

days; after two weeks, the young leave the nest. Otherwise the lifestyle is similar to that of *G. luzonica.*

Another closely related species that is very rarely imported is worth mentioning here. It is the white-breasted ground dove (*G. jobiensis*), which is only about the size of a Barbary dove and comes from New Guinea, the Bismarck Islands, Jobi, Dampier, Vulkaan, and Goodenough Islands, Samba, Solomon Islands, Vella Lavella, and Guadalcanal. Before World War II, this species was enormously popular in Europe and in the United States, and breeding successes were regularly reported. Fortunately, the popularity of this dove seems again to be on the increase. Care and breeding are similar to that described for the foregoing species. However, the species is particularly aggressive during the breeding season and this must be taken into consideration.

Genus *Goura*

In New Guinea and some adjacent islands live the three species of spectacular crowned pigeons that have become enormously popular throughout the world. They are all inhabitants of the tropical rain forest. During the day they forage on the ground for food, but at night or when danger threatens, they take to the trees. Nests are also constructed in the trees, sometimes at a great height. The main characteristic of these pigeons is, of course, their gigantic and impressive crests. They are big birds—about 5 pounds (2,500 g), with rounded wings and a medium-sized tail.

Blue-crowned Pigeon (*Goura cristata*) (2 subspecies)

Characteristics: Largely gray-blue, with part of the back and the greater and lesser wing coverts dark purple-

The Victoria crowned pigeon "will eat sliced fruits, grapes, lettuce, corn, carrots, peanuts and is especially fond of fruits of the wild fig (Ficus macrophylla)." (D. Fleay)

Imperial pigeon species are impressive but somewhat ponderous. The pied imperial pigeons are cream, silver, and white, with black on the wings and tail. They are fruit eaters, but some species extend their diets to young foilage, according to Goodwin.

red. The primaries are white with chestnut brown tips. There is a black stripe through the eyes. The beak is gray-blue, the iris ruby-colored. The large scales on the legs and feet are reddish.

Natural Range and Behavior: Northwestern New Guinea, and the islands of Misool, Salawati, Batanta, and Waigeo. They are ground-dwellers of the tropical rain forest. They feed on seeds, worms, and fruits. They are far from shy and are mediocre flyers. The hen lays a single egg that is incubated for 28 to 30 days. The young stay in the nest for about one month before fledging, then spend the nights in the nest for anoth-er one and a half months. The young are cared for by the parents for about two months!

Care and Breeding: The first specimens were brought to the Netherlands by voyagers of the East India Company, in the seventeenth century. By 1850, they were to be seen in the zoological collections of Amsterdam, Rotterdam, Antwerp, London, Paris, and Berlin. The birds quickly become tame, but are very intolerant of cold and damp. The fleshy feet are seriously affected by frostbite, even by light frosts. Most of these pigeons (particularly in public zoological collections) are therefore housed in large—minimum 24 × 24 feet (8 × 8 m)—

The maroon-breasted crowned pigeon (Goura scheepmakeri) lives in the tropical rain forests of southern New Guinea.

indoor, heated aviaries. Moreover, the aviaries are thickly planted with busy shrubs and provided with adequate, robust perches. Several pairs can be kept together. Nest foundations consist of metal baskets with a diameter of 22 inches (56 cm) and with a rim 4 inches (10 cm) high should be affixed in thick foliage and filled with grass sod, willow twigs, and straw.

In addition to a range of cereals and seeds, these exquisite pigeons should be given peas, various fruits (raisins, currants, chopped apple, pear, etc.), animal-based foods (earthworms, mealworms, canary egg food, snails, raw lean oxheart, etc.), and greens (finely chopped lettuce, endive, etc.), germinated oats and milo, chickweed, etc. Pigeon grit should be given three times a week in the mornings.

Less generally kept are the **Victoria crowned pigeon** (*G. victoria*), which is very similar to the blue-crowned species and comes from northern New Guinea and the islands of Biak and Jobi; and the **maroon-breasted crowned pigeon** (*G. scheepmakeri*) from southern New Guinea. Both species require similar care to that described for *G. cristata*.

Genus *Ducula*

Of the 39 species of fruit pigeons occurring in many parts of southern Asia, Australia, and Pacific islands, I describe only one, as the remainder are only very rarely available. Newly imported fruit pigeons are very shy at first. They require a very large aviary, especially in length—preferably at least 150 feet (50 m)—and therefore are usually kept only in zoos and bird parks.

Celebes Pied Imperial Pigeon (*Ducula luctuosa*)

Characteristics: Similar in size to a feral pigeon, it is snow-white with silver-gray primaries that are edged in black. There are a few black feathers on the belly, on the undertail coverts, and on the thighs. This is very similar in appearance to the occasionally imported pied imperial pigeon *D. bicolor,* that has black primaries with silver-gray edges and also comes from some Indonesian islands. Both of the species have a gray beak with a dark tip, a dark brown iris, and gray-blue feet. Length: 12 inches (30 cm); weight: 9¾ ounces (275 g).

Natural Range and Behavior: Celebes, Sula, Peleng, and Banggai Islands. The birds spend much time on the ground, but they must have adequate flying space in the aviary. They live mainly on the drier lowlands where there are many fruiting trees. I have also seen them at forest edges (with many berry bushes), and in cultivated areas.

Care and Breeding: This species must be kept in a roomy, high aviary that is thickly planted with shrubs. Several pairs can be kept together in such accommodations, but they must be taken to a warm spot indoors during the winter. They are fond of a sun bath, as well as a light rain shower. Unfortunately little is documented on the biology of this species. The diet should consist of chopped fruits (apples, pears, dates, soaked sultanas, apricots, figs, grapes, cherries, plums, various berries, etc.), greens (chopped lettuce, endives, chickweed, etc.), canary rearing or egg food, crumbly boiled rice, and water softened biscuit. As my friend Dr. Nicolai advises, the chopped fruits should be rolled in biscuit meal so that the pieces do not stick to each other and the birds can pick them up individually. Otherwise, the feathers around the beak are likely to get gummed up.

The bridled quail dove (Geotrygon mystacea) is closely related to the Key West quail dove (G. chrysia). The species is from the West Indies and inhabits woodland and forests.

The spectacled or white-eyed imperial pigeon (Ducula perspicillata) comes from various Moluccan islands. Both sexes are identical in color. They feed on fruits taken from branches (berries or bananas), egg food, and "hard-boiled egg yolk dipped in cream." (Dr. Heinroth, 1903)

The white-crowned pigeon (Columba leucocephala), from southern Florida, the Bahamas, the Greater and Lesser Antilles, the coast of Central America, the Yucatan, and north-western Panama, feeds on small fruits and berries, seeds, and small snails.

The Indian greenwing pigeon (Ducula aenea) inhabits forests, swamps, and open country with stands of trees. This beautiful species feeds on fruits and berries. Its clutch consists of one white egg, which is incubated for 18 days. The young leave the nest after about 20 days.

Useful Addresses and Literature

Bibliography

Goodwin, Derek: *Pigeons and Doves of the World* (3rd Edition). Cornell University Press, Ithaca, New York, 1983.

Harrison, G. J., and L. R. Harrison (eds): *Clinical Avian Medicine and Surgery*. W. B. Saunders Co., Philadelphia, Pennsylvania, 1986.

Tudor, D. C.: *Pigeon Health and Diseases*. Iowa State University Press, Ames, Iowa, 1991.

Vriends, Dr. Matthew M.: *Pigeons*. Barron's Educational Series, Inc., Hauppauge, New York, 1989.

Useful Addresses

American Dove Association
Mrs. R. Courtney, Secretary
P.O. Box 21
Milton, Kentucky 40045

American Federation of Aviculture
The A.F.A. Watchbird
P.O. Box 56218
Phoenix, Arizona 85079-6218

Association of Avian Veterinarians
5770 Lake Worth Road
Lake Worth, Florida 33463-3299

The National Pigeon Association
James R. Lairmore, Secretary
P.O. Box 3488
Orange, California 92665

World of Wings Pigeon Center
2300 N.E. 63rd
Oklahoma City, Oklahoma 73111

About the Author

Matthew M. Vriends is a Dutch-born biologist/ornithologist who holds a number of advanced degrees, including a Ph.D. in zoology. Dr. Vriends has written over eighty books in three languages on birds and other small animals. He has traveled extensively in North and South America, the United States, Africa, Australia, and Europe to observe and study birds and mammals in their natural environment and is widely regarded as an expert in tropical ornithology and aviculture. Dr. Vriends is the author or advisory editor of many of Barron's pet books.

Photo Credits

G. Ebben: front cover, inside front cover, pages 8 (two), 26, 41, 65, 97 (lower), 104 (upper), back cover.

Gary W. Ellis: pages 4, 9, 16, 22, 37, 40 (three), inside back cover.

Paula Leysen: pages 5, 12, 13, 62, 72, 77, 80, 91 (two), 94 (lower), 100, 105 (upper).

Tim Manolis: page 87 (upper).

B. Everett Webb: pages 18, 19, 30, 54, 69, 73, 82, 87 (lower), 90, 94 (upper), 97 (upper), 101, 104 (lower), 105 (lower).

Specimens courtesy of the San Diego Zoo: pages 18, 19, 30, 54, 69, 73, 97 (upper), 101, 104 (lower).

Specimens courtesy Arizona Sonoran Desert Museum: page 90.

Index

Color photos are indicated in **boldface** type.

All inquiries should be addressed to:
Barron's Educational Series, Inc.
250 Wireless Boulevard
Hauppauge, NY 11788

International Standard Book No. 0-8120-1855-9

Library of Congress Catalog Card No. 94-16574

Library of Congress Cataloging-in-Publication Data
Vriends, Matthew M., 1937–
    Doves : everything about purchase, housing, care, nutrition, breeding, and diseases : with a special chapter on understanding doves / Matthew M. Vriends ; illustrations by Tanya M. Vriends and Michele Earle-Bridges.
        p.   cm.
    Includes bibliographical references (p. 106) and index.
    ISBN 0-8120-1855-9
    1. Pigeons. I. Title.
SF465.V745   1994
636.5´96—dc20   94-16574
                                       CIP

PRINTED IN HONG KONG

19 18 17 16 15 14 13

Important Note
    The subject of this book is how to take care of various doves and pigeons in captivity. In dealing with these birds, always remember that newly purchased birds—even when they appear perfectly healthy—may well be carriers of salmonellae (see page 44). This is why it is highly advisable to have sample droppings analyzed and to observe strict hygienic rules. Other infectious diseases that can endanger humans, such as ornithosis (see page 43), are common in various doves and pigeons. If you see a doctor because you or a member of your household has symptoms of a cold or of the flu, mention that you keep doves. No one who is allergic to feathers or feather dust should keep birds. If you have any doubts, consult your physician before you buy a bird.

Front cover: White collard pigeon

Inside front cover: Laughing doves

Inside back cover: Pied collard pigeon

Back cover: Diamond doves

BARRON'S BIRD OWNER'S MANUALS AND HANDBOOKS

Barron's offers a variety of handsome and informative books on birds and bird care. Each manual and handbook has been individually written by an experienced breeder, vet, or ornithologist, and is filled with full-color photos and instructive, high-quality line art. You'll find everything you need to know about feeding, caging, breeding, and keeping healthy and contented birds.

Owner's Manuals:

African Gray Parrots
ISBN 0-8120-3773-1

Amazon Parrots
ISBN 0-7641-1036-5

Canaries
ISBN 0-7641-0936-7

Cockatiels
ISBN 0-7641-0938-3

Cockatoos
ISBN 0-7641-1037-3

Conures
ISBN 0-7641-1038-1

Doves
ISBN 0-8120-1855-9

Feeding and Sheltering Backyard Birds
ISBN 0-8120-4252-2

Feeding and Sheltering European Birds
ISBN 0-8120-2858-9

Gouldian Finches
ISBN 0-8120-4523-8

Long-Tailed Parakeets
ISBN 0-8120-1351-4

Lories and Lorikeets
ISBN 0-8120-1567-3

Lovebirds
ISBN 0-8120-9014-4

Macaws
ISBN 0-8120-4768-0

Mynahs
ISBN 0-8120-3688-3

Parakeets
ISBN 0-7641-1032-2

Parrots
ISBN 0-8120-4823-7

Pigeons
ISBN 0-8120-4044-9

Zebra Finches
ISBN 0-7641-1040-3

Handbooks:

The New Australian Parakeet Handbook
ISBN 0-8120-4739-7

The New Bird Handbook
ISBN 0-8120-4157-7

The New Canary Handbook
ISBN 0-8120-4879-2

The Cockatiel Handbook
ISBN 0-7641-1017-9

The New Finch Handbook
ISBN 0-8120-2859-7

The Parrotlet Handbook
ISBN 0-7641-0962-6

The Parakeet Handbook
ISBN 0-7641-1018-7

The New Parrot Handbook
ISBN 0-8120-3729-4

The New Softbill Handbook
ISBN 0-8120-4075-9

Books may be purchased at your local bookstore, or by mail from Barron's. Enclose check or money order for the total amount plus sales tax where applicable and 18% for postage and handling (minimum charge $5.95). Prices subject to change without notice.

Barron's Educational Series, Inc.
250 Wireless Blvd., Hauppauge, NY 11788 • To order toll-free: 1-800-645-3476
In Canada: Georgetown Book Warehouse • 34 Armstrong Ave.,
Georgetown, Ont. L7G 4R9 • Order toll-free in Canada: 1-800-247-7160
Or order from your favorite bookstore or pet store
Visit our web site at: www.barronseduc.com

(62b) 12/99